The Covenant of Peace

Shawn Saunders

Published by:

 **Seraph Books**

www.seraphbooks.com

–Copyright © 2014, Shawn Saunders

All rights reserved. Printed and bound in the United States of America. No part of this book may be reproduced or transmitted in any form by any means, electronic or mechanical, including photocopying, recording, or by an information storage and retrieval system --- without permission in writing from the publisher, except by a reviewer, who may quote brief passages in a review.

Published by: Seraph Books, LLC.

Scripture quotations are taken from the Holy Bible, New Living Translation, copyright ©1996, 2004, 2007, 2013 by Tyndale House Foundation. Used by permission of Tyndale House Publishers, Inc., Carol Stream, Illinois 60188. All rights reserved.

Cover Design By: Alyssa M. Curry
Copyediting: Alyssa M. Curry
Author Photo: Imagery by Jules Photography

ISBN Hardcover: 978-0-9911760-6-9
ISBN Paperback: 978-0-9911760-7-6
ISBN E-book: 978-0-9911760-8-3
Library of Congress Control Number: 2014934833

For information regarding special discounts for bulk purchases of this book for educational, gift purposes, as a charitable donation, or to arrange a speaking event, please visit: www.seraphbooks.com
www.shawn-saunders.com
twitter@saunders40
www.facebook.com/shawn.saunders.1671

Dedication

This book is dedicated to God in whom I live, breathe and have my being, the very essence of who I am. Without You I am nothing. Thank You for trusting me with such an important message. May I always strive to please only You.

To my children, Kristen and Christina. My passionate love for both of you is the driving force behind my determination to lead by example. In both of you I find my strength. Because of you, I am **Moving in 3-D®**.

Acknowledgements

To the numerous teachers and leaders whose wisdom and correction helped to awaken the gifts God placed in me, especially Apostle Colamae Collymore.

Aunt Virginia your words of wisdom released me to finally live in total obedience to God. Thanks for believing and supporting me.

Uncle Randolph your understanding and forgiveness opened the door for God to truly use and bless me. I cannot thank you enough.

To my friends and family who obliged me with their time and patience while listening to the fountain that flowed as God began to develop me.

To my pastors, Bishop Henry and Pastor Carol Fernandez, I want to say thank you for the gifts of favor and access to your lives and ministry. For giving me a platform to exercise the call of God on my life and being excellent examples of what faith in God can do.

A Note To The Reader

As you read through the pages of this book, I encourage you to open your heart and mind to the knowledge God wants you to receive. Try not to take every piece of this book to heart but pay attention to the part that speaks specifically to you. Read from the perspective that God cares about every part of you. He wants you to experience balance and fulfillment in every area of your life despite what the world system may say. He wants you to know that He will never stop loving and caring for you.

Introduction

Arriving to the point of writing and even publishing this book was a tremendous journey of desire and determination. My desire and passion is to always be obedient to the plans and intent of God for my life. Over the years I developed a strong determination to accept and complete every assignment I was given. However, the discipline required to complete this book was tested over and over again in my obedience to God versus my willingness to go against religious norms. Observing and being a part of a culture that has dropped the ball on caring for their own, it no longer became an option but a mandate to be a part of the solution rather than turn a blind eye to the problem. The people have cried out to God for help and He wants them to know that He heard and He cares enough to answer.

Understanding divinely how much we are meant to prosper during our lifetime, I accepted this opportunity to use my life as an example to bring a realistic perspective to what God intends for each of us who would choose to believe Him and practice His principles.

The covenant of peace is intended to give you a modern view of how words spoken by God thousands of years ago are still relevant today. Its purpose is for you to see yourself as a part of the covenant and know that your success is already guaranteed. God is the same as yesterday, today and forever. The Bible reminds us that we perish for no other reason than the lack of knowledge. What you know and believe will make the difference in your life.

Chapter One

Do You Know? Do You Believe?

Throughout my journey I've chosen to dedicate my life to such an amazing and awesome God who rules supreme with all the power in Heaven and Earth. He has the entire world at His command yet; He knows my name, address and even the number of strands of hair on my head. God took time out of His busy schedule to create me as a unique being, placed me in a beautiful, healthy body and designed a life plan just for me. He has given me access to His throne. I can call on Him anytime and He will answer, making certain that I never feel alone. He has assigned an entourage of bodyguards and a team of personal assistants to handle all of my requests. He increases my wisdom, knowledge and understanding daily. And, when I mess up, He gives me another day to get it right. This very God, who sacrificed His only son so I could have a chance to live, gave His son to me as my master intercessor.

I have discovered that I am special to God. He created me in His image and has chosen me to represent Him on this earth. But the discovery doesn't end there. What I've established is that in His eyes, God created all of us special. I am one of His children. And, like any good parent, He has a plan for every one of us and intends to keep His promise.

On this journey of discovery, I've found that many Christians did not fully understand who and what they are in Christ. Most have yet to comprehend their purpose for being on this earth and struggle to find their place in this world. Many are living defeated, broken lives without hope of how to begin the process of finding God.

My focus is to create an atmosphere that will allow you to understand the word of God. This perspective will reveal what God wants to do for you along your journey and what He wants to do by working through you. I would like to take you on a journey with the intent to free your mind to accept the fact that God placed all of us here as vessels for the purpose of completing His plan on this earth. It will be a journey that will take you down a path filled with memories that may evoke past pains and internal struggles. However, it will cause you to recognize the matters of the heart, mind, soul and body, which may have hindered you from becoming all that God created you to be. We begin the journey of getting set to receive not only the goodness of God but also becoming a weapon for retrieving territory lost to the enemy.

In a study published in the United States in 2003 it was discovered that there were huge disparities between the finances of various religions: Baptist, and Jehovah's witnesses were at the lower end, Jews were at the highest end and we, the modern or charismatic fell in the middle. Now what would be the reason for this? It's easy to say that the Jews are God's chosen people and so are blessed more than us because of it. However, not all Jews are wealthy. So how would you explain that? We are descendants of Abraham and joint heirs in the Kingdom of God. We are children of the Most High God who owns the cattle on a thousand hills. God promises to supply all of our needs according to His riches in glory. Give and you shall receive good measure, pressed down shaken together and running over. If we believe this why are we still trying to survive rather than living prosperous productive lives? Something is missing in the equation and it all comes down to what is in our hearts and minds.

The prosperity of His people is so important to God that He thought it necessary to establish a covenant with Himself to ensure every person who believes in Him and exercise His principles inherits the right to prosper. In fact, prosperity and all the elements that go along with it are referenced in the Bible more times than salvation. While it is extremely essential that we secure our relationship with God through our confession of sins and acceptance of Jesus Christ as our Lord and Savior, this eternal salvation is not something we have to work for. There is absolutely nothing we can do to obtain salvation other than to believe in the Lord Jesus Christ. Jesus did all of the work when He died on the cross.

Although God in His good pleasure to prosper us established a covenant to ensure it, there is no guarantee that all who believes will actually experience the covenant of peace in their lifetime. The reason for this is the requirement of actions on our part. So in order to enjoy the benefits of the covenant of peace, one would have to know and implement the terms of the covenant.

Most of the covenants outlined in the Bible were between God and man. In each instance, there were three elements or components of that covenant. These are the promises, terms and a seal thereby making it a binding and unbreakable commitment for both parties involved.

Let us look at the covenant God made with a man named Abraham. In the book of Genesis, God made a covenant with Abraham in which He promised to bless and multiply Abraham and his descendants for generations. He promises that He will bless everyone who blesses Abraham and curse those who curse him. Through Abraham, all the nations of the world would be blessed. God made these promises but along with it certain conditions or terms that Abraham had to follow. Abraham demonstrated his agreement with this covenant by circumcising himself and all the males under his leadership. This circumcision represented the shedding of blood and sealing the covenant forever (Genesis 17:1-14).

God also made a covenant by Himself. In Jeremiah 31:31 He spoke of establishing a new covenant. This covenant became the promise of salvation to all men and the eventual birth, death and resurrection of the Messiah, Jesus Christ. It established our ability to inherit eternal life for both Jews and Gentiles. Christians live under the new covenant believing that Jesus Christ is the Messiah and that the only way to the Father is through Jesus Christ (Matthew 26:27-28). The promise is eternal salvation for all men. The terms are that you accept His son, Jesus Christ and believe in Him. As a reward, you will inherit eternal life.

What's interesting is that at the time God established this covenant with Himself, He set the promises and the terms but there was no seal by the shedding of blood. This did not come until later when Jesus was scourged, pierced and nailed to the cross. Repeatedly Jesus's blood was shed to ensure the unbreakable seal of the new covenant.

The same is true of the covenant of peace. Again, God established a covenant by himself (Ezekiel 34:25). God made promises of a shepherd coming to watch over His sheep to ensure certain blessings. As a result there are a number of terms we, the sheep, must follow in order to receive the blessings of the covenant of peace. However, this covenant was not sealed right away. The seal through the shedding of blood never came until the shedding of the blood of Jesus Christ, our ultimate Shepherd.

In previous covenants between God and man, the man would seal the covenant with blood by sacrificing an animal at the end of the transaction. This seal with blood meant the covenant could not be broken. When you look at the covenant of peace, in Ezekiel 34:23-24, as God is speaking He says that He will send David to be a shepherd over His flock and feed them. In addition, He said that David would be a prince amongst the people.

The Bible gives an account of David as a shepherd boy who later became king over Israel. He fought many battles protecting the people of Israel and left a legacy of being a great King with whom God was extremely pleased. So, if David were a king how would he be a prince? At the time Ezekiel received this revelation from God, David was long dead. Why then would God say that David would be the Shepherd and a prince? Or was He speaking of a direct descendant of David?

Jesus is a direct descendant of the genealogy of David. He is often referred to as the son of David, Prince of Peace and the Good Shepherd. He came into this world through the bloodline of David and became the sacrificial Lamb for a people whom God loved so much. The shedding of Jesus' blood sealed the covenant of peace and all other covenants God made by Himself. Luke 22:20 states, "This cup is the new covenant between God and His people—an agreement confirmed with my blood, which is poured out as a sacrifice for you." This made each covenant irrevocable for eternity. He is our Shepherd. He is our Prince of Peace. Through Jesus Christ, as His people and the sheep of His pasture, we can boldly claim the blessings of not only eternal life but also the covenant of peace.

Before Jesus came, man operated under a curse of having to work for a living. This curse stemmed from the Garden of Eden when Adam and Eve disobeyed God and ate from the tree of the knowledge of good and evil. Unless God himself supernaturally blessed the people, all other increase was obtained through some form of work. At the exodus out of Egypt, God instructed the children of Israel to borrow gold and other items from the Egyptians to take with them into the desert. Even though it may appear they borrowed from the Egyptians, God was making sure they received payment for the many years of free labor the children of Israel had provided. So they toiled and were able to eat while in Egypt but by taking the gold from the Egyptians, they were reimbursed for their years of unpaid labor.

It is not until the arrival of Jesus and the shedding of His blood that it became possible for man to receive what he did not work for. In Luke 6:38 it states, "Give, and you shall receive. Your gift will return to you in full—pressed down, shaken together to make room for more, running over, and poured into your lap. The amount you give will determine the amount you get back." It does not say that you had to work but the requirement was to give. The more you give, the more you will receive.

If God had already cursed the ground and said that by the sweat of our brows we would eat bread, how can we receive abundant blessings by just giving? It would have to mean that the curse was broken from over all humanity. This happened through Jesus Christ.

In Genesis it says that when God cursed the ground, thorns and thistles came up as a sign that the ground was cursed. In the New Testament, on His way to Calvary, the soldiers mocked Jesus and placed a crown of thorns on His head calling Him King of the Jews. Some believe they were the same type of thorns that came up in the Garden of Eden. Whether this is true or not, what stands out to me is that as those thorns were pressed onto the head of Jesus and ripping into His flesh, blood starting dripping down His face. With the curse came thorns and with thorns and the blood of Jesus the curse of poverty was broken. This cleared the way for every believer to freely accept the covenant of peace in his or her life. Jesus our Shepherd, the Sacrificial Lamb established the covenant through His blood, death and resurrection. Hallelujah!!

In Hebrew 8:6 we read of how Jesus mediates a new covenant for us. This confirms that not only the Jews are the blessed people of God, but everyone who accepts Jesus as the Messiah. We no longer have to repeatedly make sacrifices to God as under the old covenants, we have Jesus who made the one sacrifice for all sins (Hebrews 10:1-10).

Chapter Two

A Call to Accountability

In the book of Ezekiel 34:25-31, God speaks of establishing a covenant of peace for His sheep or rather the people who He loves. This covenant of peace outlines the blessings God will bestow upon His loved ones.

What's interesting is how this covenant came to be established. Ezekiel 34:1-24 begins with God directly speaking to the shepherds letting them know of His displeasure in the way in which they were treating the sheep that were placed under their care. It is without question that God was speaking at the time, to leaders who were placed in positions of authority over the children of Israel. Here, God expresses His disappointment that the leaders had taken the best the land had produced for themselves and failed to care for the people under their authority. He scolded them about the fact that they ate the best of the meat and caused the sheep to scatter. He also scolded the sheep who drank clean water then expected others to drink after the water was muddied. He spoke of their lack of attention to the fact that the sick, broken, and lost were not cared for. They were abandoned to look after themselves. As a result, wild animals attacked and destroyed many.

In this chapter, God outlined his frustration with the shepherds and was emphatic in letting them know that He was removing them from their positions as shepherds and would replace them with a shepherd (God himself) who would care for his sheep. He later says (Ezekiel 34:23) it would be David. The alternation between God, David and the Shepherd implies that they may all be one.

These scriptures resonate clearly in today's society. Many leaders, secular and religious, seek after personal gain instead of fulfilling the role of protector and advocate of the people placed under their leadership. There are a plethora of leaders increasing their personal wealth and pleasure at the expense of people who trust in them for guidance and protection.

Unfortunately, this is true within the church. In our daily lives, we watch as the leaders (apostles, prophets, pastors, evangelist, etc.) implement strategies to increase their personal possessions and wealth, while the members of their congregation suffer under the burden of financial, spiritual, professional and emotional bondage. They have placed tremendous pressure on their members to be supportive of their ministries, without any return of investment into the people God placed in their care.

Over the years, I've had the opportunity to speak with a number of people who have expressed their disillusion with church because of negative experiences. Some have listened to and obeyed leaders who gave them specific instructions on how much money they were to give to the advancement of ministries. They were told "Obey God and give ... " specifying an amount followed by, "And God will bless you in ... " providing a specific number of days.

Because of the fear of disobedience to God, many of these people have given the last of their earnings only to end up broke and without fulfillment of the promise of a blessing in the number of days stated. They were left to wonder if the word was really from God or not. When confronted, many leaders invoke feelings of guilt on the part of the church members making them feel that they are to blame if God did not bless them.

As we examine the cry of the people across many denominations, the common voice is one of deprivation and lack of direction in the matters that would seemingly make lives easier. There has been tremendous emphasis placed on giving tithes, offerings, volunteering and so forth. However, very little investment is made in ensuring the members are taught the word of God in a manner that will allow practical application in current times.

Members are bombarded with the biblical principal of tithing so that God can meet all of their needs. They are not taught to understand how God will actually make that happen for them. There is considerable emphasis placed on the significance and act of giving. Unfortunately, there is not enough on the importance of receiving or rather the need to expect to receive a harvest.

It's disheartening to observe many dedicated people going to church on a regular basis giving as instructed from the pulpit. Yet, they are constantly dealing with the reality of watching their finances dwindle as the financial situation of their leadership increases. They are faced with being devoured by the world's economic system of hunger, foreclosures, and repossessions while remaining unable to meet their basic human needs. As they continue, or begin to struggle, their leadership is growing financially stronger daily. These people would rather starve than withhold their donations to the church. But, at the end of the day, in this world that we live in, outside of the church, the sheep are defenseless among the wild animals of the financial spectrum.

The study published in 2003 demonstrated what we can clearly observe across many religions with poverty at its highest among the members of churches. The study stated religion is the number one influencer of a person's perception of wealth, education, family, and work. If this is true, then what is the church teaching its people, that so many of them live in poverty?

Over the years, many churches have placed emphasis on sin, repentance, humility, wrath of God, the need to give to the church, and evangelizing the world for Christ. However, there has not been enough teaching on a positive approach to wealth accumulation despite there being more scriptural references to prosperity than there are to salvation. There are generations of Christians who don't believe that God wants them to be blessed in all aspects of their lives. They cannot wrap their minds around the fact that God established a covenant with Himself to guarantee that they are blessed in an excessive manner. To speak of such matters to most Christians is considered blasphemy at the highest end of the continuum and greed at the lower end.

Why is that? The words of the Bible are there for everyone to read. In fact, the Bible has always been a bestselling book. So, if it is a bestseller, are people actually reading it? Are people understanding what it says about past, present and future life? What are leaders teaching their followers about this book that is a road map to the blessings of God? According to Psalms 109:10, the word of God is given as a lamp to guide our steps and show us the pathway we should follow as we go about our daily lives.

What are leaders teaching in regards to the blessings of God as it applies to wealth and prosperity? Truth be told, not much. The majority of leaders can effectively speak on the need for tithes and offerings but they aren't knowledgeable about the biblical principles as it applies to financial peace. More Christians are looking forward to their heavenly home in the sky. They can't embrace a piece of heaven here on earth because of the hell they are living daily.

What has become evident is that the knowledge of leadership, in regards to what the word of God says about prosperity, is scanty at best. Most leaders don't fully understand the Bible and its connections from Genesis to Revelation. There are many leaders who have never read the Bible from Genesis to Revelation, because it's easier to concentrate on the portions of the Bible that relate to their "calling." They are neglecting to obtain a global view of a God who is compassionate, omnipotent, omniscient and infinite. Sadly, many views and opinions of leaders on wealth and prosperity have been passed down to them from either their parents or other leaders who may have preceded them. Hence, their ideals and opinions are based in human error rather than the factual word of God. Without adequate knowledge of the blessings of God, how can a leader instruct and guide members to a life they themselves don't fully understand? How can they lead their members or sheep into a lifestyle that they haven't experienced and can't imagine themselves living? It may surprise some that these leaders who lack the knowledge and training to teach their followers are usually the very ones who highly criticize those that put their reputations on the line to teach on the topic of prosperity. They categorize it as the "prosperity gospel" when prosperity is only a large part of one gospel.

On one of my many business trips, I sat next to a pastor on a flight that took just over an hour. During this time, we spoke about the Bible, the fact that he was a pastor, and his understanding of many things in the Bible. I was shocked to hear him say that he had not read the entire Bible from Genesis to Revelation. The most inconceivable admission occurred when he casually explained that he didn't fully understand the Bible nor had he experienced an intimate relationship with God, the presence of the Holy Spirit. I remember sitting there and wondering "Why and how did you become a pastor without knowing the very foundation of what you are supposed to believe?" Here was a man leading a congregation without knowing where he was going. Amazing! He was handicapped in teaching his people because he lacked the foundational knowledge necessary to provide guidance.

There are a lot of us operating in positions of leadership with very little knowledge of the word or power of God. Sadly, there are many people who are living their lives based on what little they are taught rather than the full scope of who God really is. Whatever the preacher teaches is all they know. Granted, knowledge of God is a continuous learning process, which requires constant reading of the Bible.

No one person has all of the answers or fully understands the ways of God. On the other hand, there are leaders who fully comprehend that God wants His people to be blessed. They understand the word, have implemented it in their lives and are now living with the rewards of following biblical principles. They are living examples of how God wants His people to be blessed. However, some of these leaders have taken this knowledge, hoarded it for themselves and used it to exploit the ignorance and generosity of their followers. Instead of investing the time and resources into ensuring the people they are responsible for are taught how to prosper, they exhaust the little resources of the people and leave them to their own devises. As a result, their members are sinking deeper and deeper into debt, depression and walking away from God. After all, who wants to serve a God that lets people suffer? Who wants to serve a God who only allows certain people to prosper while the rest live a daily life of neglect and pain?

This group of leaders are the shepherds God is referring to in Ezekiel 34:1-24. These are the people who are guilty of taking the best for themselves. They look after their own affairs while their followers are left to wander in a world of financial, spiritual, psychological, and physical mayhem. They have allowed their followers to be swallowed up in a world that has placed much emphasis on profit at the expense of whatever and whomever. These leaders are experiencing a piece of heaven, while here on earth, as they prepare for their heavenly home. Meanwhile, their followers are experiencing hell on earth and yearning for their home in the sky.

In Ezekiel 34:2-4, God clearly instructs Ezekiel to prophesy against the shepherds, "... What sorrow awaits you shepherds who feed yourselves instead of your flock. Shouldn't shepherds feed their sheep? You drink the milk, wear the wool, and butcher the best animals, but you let your flocks starve. You have not taken care of the weak. You have not tended the sick or bound up the injured. You have not gone looking for those who have wandered away and are lost. Instead, you have ruled them with harshness and cruelty." God goes on to say in verse 10 "... I now consider these shepherds my enemies, and I will hold them responsible for what has happened to my flock. I will take away their right to feed the flock, and I will stop them from feeding themselves. I will rescue my flock from their mouths; the sheep will no longer be their prey."

Leaders are being called to accountability to God for the manner in which they oversee the people under their care. In this season, God is saying that those leaders, who don't take their positions seriously and perform their responsibilities with diligence and integrity, will be stopped and removed by God having their rights to leadership revoked. God hears the cries of His people and He will rescue them.

Chapter Three

The Intent of Peace

God has determined that He will come to the rescue of His people. In Ezekiel 34:22-23 God says, "So I will rescue my flock, and they will no longer be abused. I will judge between one animal of the flock and another. And I will set over them one shepherd, my servant David. He will feed them and be a shepherd to them." Practically speaking in modern times, clearly this shepherd cannot be the physical David but rather a descendant of David. So for us this shepherd that God sent into the world to feed His sheep and be a shepherd to them is Jesus Christ, the Son of the Living God. David is quoted in Psalms 100:3 as saying, "...we are His people, the sheep of his pasture."

Having established that God considers us His sheep and Jesus Christ came to this earth to be our shepherd, what then is the blessing or reward of having a shepherd appointed by God?

In the scriptures, God states that He will establish a covenant of peace with His people. This covenant incorporates a number of blessings from God himself.

God says He will (Ezekiel 34:25-31):

1) Drive away the dangerous animals from the land;
2) Bless His people and their homes;
3) Send the showers needed in the proper season;
4) Shower down the blessings (showers of blessings);
5) Cause the orchards and fields to yield bumper crops;
6) Make their land famous for its crop;
7) Break the chains of slavery and rescue from those who enslave.

These seven blessings may not appear to be a covenant of peace at first glance. However, when you examine each of the components of the covenant, they collectively represent peace. Peace of mind, body and spirit. When your physical, psychological, financial, and spiritual needs are met satisfactorily, you enter a place of peace in your life. This would then be a fulfillment of the covenant of peace.

To be at peace is to be quiet or tranquil, mentally calm and serene, free from war, violence and disturbance. **The Hebrew word for peace is shalom, which has additional meanings such as to be happy, well and healthy along with prosperous.** Each meaning had its significance, but shalom represents effectively the kind of peace mentioned in the covenant of peace. God intends for us to have freedom from disturbance but He also wants us to prosper and be healthy.

What is a covenant? *A covenant is an agreement that is binding. It is a formal contract between two people, a pledge, bargain and a promise.*

I am going to refer to God's covenant as a promise. A promise God has made to His people. A promise made by God that is backed by the full authority of His grace. A covenant is not meant to be broken. So when God makes a covenant either with man or with Himself, it is especially important to know that it is a promise that cannot, ever be broken.

Numbers 23:19 says "God is not a man, so he does not lie. He is not human, so he does not change his mind. Has he ever spoken and failed to act? Has he ever *promised* and not carried it through?"

God fulfills every promise He has ever made. This is evident through the many covenants God made with men such as Adam, Abraham, Moses, Noah and others. It is through His covenant with Abraham that we, who are considered Gentiles, gained access to the covenant blessings God spoke to Abraham and his descendants. God is still keeping His promise to Abraham to this day. Jews and Gentiles, the ones who embrace the promises and commandments of God, are both increasing daily under the Abrahamic covenant established thousands of years ago. Suffice it to say, He is a God of His word. If He says it, He will do it.

If God says He promises to do the seven items listed as part of the covenant of peace, we should then expect that He will do what He says. The benefits of believing God in this covenant are outlined in Ezekiel 34:25-31.

You will be able to:

1) Live in safety (camp safely in the wildest places and sleep in the woods without fear);
2) No longer be prey for other nations;
3) No longer be devoured by wild animals;
4) Never again suffer from famines;
5) Never again suffer from insults of foreign nations;
6) Be famous for your crops;
7) Know that He is your God and He is with you.

In the pages to follow, I will go over each component of the covenant and describe it as it applies to our times and its relevance in our lives.

Chapter Four

Promises of the Covenant of Peace

DRIVE AWAY THE DANGEROUS ANIMALS FROM THE LAND

In Biblical times the scriptures mention there was a threat that wild animals would eat the flocks of sheep, goats and cattle. As a result, there were shepherds whose job it was to guard the animals and drive away or kill the animals that threatened the herd. Oftentimes, the herd didn't even know the danger was present. The battle was between the shepherd and the enemy; the predatory animal. This prevented loss of animals in addition to loss of income. It meant that the wild animals developed a sense of fear for the territories that were guarded and would then go off to hunt in less protected areas.

As the shepherd over His flock, God is saying that He will cover us under His protection. He will stand guard for the dangers that could destroy us during our lifetime. He will stand against every attack of the enemy. He will fight our battles even when we don't realize we need protecting. He will be the one to identify every situation and circumstance that would cause us harm. But most importantly, He will send our enemies away in such a manner that they will never want to attack again. The enemy will understand not to tread on the territory of the covenant people of God. God will drive away the dangers that could consume us and provide an environment of safety.

To have the divine protection of God means that no weapon formed against the covenant one or their home will prosper or stand and all who will open their mouth to judge are already condemned. It means to live under the full protection of Psalms 91. God has you in His secret place, under His shadow. The enemy can't come near you even if they could find you.

"The Lord's light penetrates the human spirit, exposing every hidden motive" Proverbs 20:27. Only God knows the true thoughts and motives of people. Through situations and circumstances, He will allow people to reveal who they genuinely are so you can take protective measures.

Bless His People and Their Homes

The act of God protecting us from any danger that can destroy us is a tremendous blessing by itself. But God takes it even further. He determines to bless His people and their homes.

To grant a favor or to consecrate something to another person is considered a blessing. Most blessings come as a result of an individual granting favor or a blessing on another. With such an act one can be considered to be blessed or in a state of prosperity and happiness. In most instances in the Bible, the one giving the blessing is God Himself.

To be blessed by God is to have the favor of God on your life. In Ezekiel 34, God is saying that He will not only bless you but also your home. This includes your family and all of your possessions. You and your family will live in a state of perpetual blessings from God.

Knowing that the Master Himself has chosen to bless and favor me is my peace. That means no human can reverse the blessing God has placed on my life.

You will experience happiness in relationships, marriage, children, friends and relatives. Your children and grandchildren will increase and they will be at peace with you. Not only is every part of your body and possessions blessed, but you will have time to enjoy the blessings of God.

SEND THE SHOWERS NEEDED IN THE PROPER SEASON

In my limited knowledge of farming, I understand that there is a time in which a farmer must prepare the ground for planting. He then has to plant his seeds at a specific time then wait for the rains to come so the seeds can germinate and start to grow. The process of producing a harvest covers a period of time that requires showers or rain to come at different intervals for each stage of the crop.

Substantial rain, too early, could cause the crop to go bad. On the other hand, too little rain could stunt the growth of the crop and decrease the harvest or cause no harvest at all. It's a delicate balance of the rain coming at the right time and in the right quantity to produce bountiful harvests.

In this covenant blessing, God is telling His people that He will send the showers (rain) at the right time and for the length of time required to produce a bountiful harvest. The first rain is to initiate the growth process. The second rain increases the growth. The latter rain is to mature the crop and prepare for the harvest. Lack of adequate rain at any of these steps or too much rain could destroy the entire crop and abort the harvest intended.

Having the showers fall on your field of planted seeds at the right time and in the right quantity guarantees an abundant harvest from God.

Shower Down The Blessings

As a little girl we sang this song "Showers of blessing, showers of blessing we need. Mercy drops round us are falling but for the showers we need." I remember singing it many times over and over again but never really knew what it meant. As the Lord began to deal with me on this topic, I did my due diligence and looked up the words. A shower is a substantial but brief rain, which can be sudden and unanticipated. It can also be a significant amount of things occurring at the same time. This may include gifts given to a person all at the same time.

Under the covenant of peace God is promising that He will shower down the blessings upon us. He will cause sudden, large outpouring of blessings to come to us. He will also cause sudden, intermittent outpouring of favor to come into our lives. We will experience what it means to live under an open heaven as stated in Malachi 3:10 where He says try Him and see if He won't open the windows of heaven pouring out a blessing that you won't have enough space to receive.

To have showers of blessings upon your life and at the right season means that there is never, ever going to be a time in your life when the provisions of God are not evident and tangible. You will never experience lack. Your needs and wants will be met. He is Lord of the harvest. He controls the showers. He controls the harvest. And He, God Himself, is saying that He will favor (bless) you under His covenant of peace.

CAUSE THE ORCHARDS AND FIELDS TO YIELD BUMPER CROPS

An orchard is a mass area of land in which large quantities of a particle type of fruit bearing trees are planted. Apples are usually planted in orchards as well as other fruits such as pears and peaches along with others. It's a beautiful sight when you're driving by one, especially during the time of blossoms and just before harvesting. Imagine your field or orchard being larger than any other. Then imagine the most incredible quality of fruit in terms of size, color and juicy goodness. You hoped for a harvest but this is beyond human imagination. Wow! Looking back years later, you're still talking about that year when you had the greatest harvest of your life. That was a great year, in fact, the best ever. Now, imagine that every year for generations, your harvest is continuously beyond your imagination. Your harvest exceeds all others. This is God's promise of a bumper crop.

The same applies to the person who is a professional, has a career, job, the investor, inventor and even the business owner. God will increase your harvest (product) to a level it exceeds all others in your area of expertise. Revelations and inventive ideas will develop into valuable commodities for you. Your gifts and talents that you foster will now be protected, developed, nurtured and brought to fruition by God. What an amazing promise from God. It's impossible for you to fail.

God recognizes that our human nature requires reward. We are built to expect appreciation and recognition for the work and good things we do. When we don't receive these, gradually our actions become laborious tasks rather than acts of kindness and pleasure. We sometimes become discouraged and often wander away from our jobs, careers and religious organizations only to find ourselves away from hope, away from God.

God is promising us that He will not only give us a harvest but He will produce a bumper crop. Again, for those of us who aren't farmers, this may have little meaning. But farmers understand that a bumper crop means that your harvest is exceptionally large, fine and successful. Your harvest has exceeded the produce of all other farmers and is in a league of its own. There's nothing that can compare to it. It is so obvious that everyone can see it. Because of its size, quality, and especially its difference, everyone wants it. Value and demand is now within your field. Quality drives demand and demand drives value or income. God is promising all of this to you. You will be most successful in your career, business and all the works of your hands. Whatever you have chosen to invest into will result in bountiful results.

Make Their Land Famous For Its Crop

Because of the exceptional quality and quantity of your produce (harvest), your value increases. In addition, your name becomes known throughout the land and even the world because of what you produce. People everywhere are talking about you; describing you as the best at what you do. Along comes notoriety, which results in a platform that allows you to now make a difference for God on this earth.

In present day, this not only applies to the farmer but also to:

1) The employee who becomes most valued for their skills;
2) The professional who stands out from the rest because of the problems they solve for others;
3) The inventor, whose ideas meet the needs of people on a global scale;

4) The business owner, whose company is in high demand because of the type of services provided;
5) The philanthropist or developer who does what others only dream of;
6) And of course, the stay-at-home parent who has the time and resources to spend investing into teaching their children to be world changers for the kingdom of God.

BREAK THE CHAINS OF SLAVERY AND RESCUE FROM THOSE WHO ENSLAVE

All of the elements of the covenant of peace are relatively easy to understand but having someone grasp "chains of slavery" becomes a little more complicated. In our mind's eye we see images of the slave man or woman being towered over by their masters. Often, we can envision the crack of the whip, pain, suffering and wounds that are too deep to heal by any human hands. The short of it is that for those of us who have experienced this or even are descendants of slaves; the memories are often vivid and unsettling. To think that in this modern day, some of us are still enslaved is considered inhumane and calls for immediate and drastic action. Often, activist groups champion the cause to set people free from slavery. Some have even funded organizations that buy people out of slavery. These are all very real experiences that require intervention from people who are determined and organizations that have made it their mandate to abolish slavery globally.

Within the very walls of our own society, there is another form of slavery that is progressive and invasive. It has become like a cancer that has taken over groups of people for whom it requires God's intervention. This form of slavery is the most crippling because it takes over every aspect of an individual's life. It dominates, overpowers, beats, threatens and separates, causing wounds that no human can heal. It is so elusive in its operations that many don't even recognize its presence. When threatened with exposure, there's a media storm of verbiage to protect its operations. Quietly it moves through society enslaving one person at a time. Its grip has become so strong that the few who recognize and expose its ugliness become targets of attacks and denigration.

Believe it or not, this form of slavery exists, even in your home. Every day of your life, you deal with its tentacles that have managed to permeate the very fiber of society, culture, race, religion and ethnicity. When targeted by the few activists, the ugliness of prejudice raises its head in the form of anger and resentment. And, just as prejudice amongst race and ethnicity has caused anger, hatred and separation, this too has caused great division among the different religions. Surprisingly, more religious leaders invest in spending time trying to protect this type of slavery than they would spend learning how to eradicate it. Could it be that they themselves are enslaved as well?

The slavery I am speaking of is poverty. The presence of poverty is a clear indication of the absence of the covenant of peace in that area of a person's life. Poverty not only applies to the lack of finances but also to a lack of knowledge, health (physical and emotional), spiritual clarity, and understanding of the word of God. I've learned a great deal from my experiences throughout the years. I've discovered that any area of your life in which you are not equipped to effectively handle matters that arise, indicates lack and illuminates the presence of poverty in health, education, relationships or finances. If you aren't balanced or fully equipped in an area, you are experiencing poverty in that matter.

While poverty at its core is spiritually based, it's also a mindset. It's an acceptance of a belief system that governs the actions you take in your daily life that leads to a lifestyle of deprivation. The poverty mindset determines what decisions you make when faced with situations regarding finances, education, health, having children, employment, religion, and relationships. What we believe to be true is a key factor in how we will make choices regarding our lives. As a result, people who have spiritual freedom from poverty can still have a mindset of poverty that causes them to make bad decisions in specific areas of their lives. Spiritually they are free, but not in their minds.

A lot of people have been taught that to be poor is acceptable. As a child, my mother would say "Poorness is no disgrace," and I would add, "But it is an inconvenience." Some Christians believe that to live in lack is acceptable in the eyes of God. They adopt the mentality that if God wants me to have it, He will give it to me. Others believe that it is honorable to live in poverty as well as a sign of humility and their reward is stored up for them in heaven. To want a piece of heaven while here on earth is ungodly. Most don't realize that true peace on earth, living under the covenant of peace, requires balance in all areas of our lives.

Along with other religions, some churches have played a major role in teaching a false belief system that to be prosperous is a sin. They have placed a lot of emphasis on only the financial aspect leaving a void in several other areas where education is needed. Over generations they have taught people that to be rich is not a good thing because it's easier for a camel to go through the eye of a needle than for a rich man to enter the kingdom of God. Hence, a lot of Christians fear wealth and are quite content to live as beggars or at the mercy of God rather than implement strategies to increase the quality and worth of their lives through education, careers, businesses, or investments.

This mentality has become the strongest, and biggest invasion of slavery that goes undocumented daily. This form of mental slavery is so pervasive; it has become one of the most challenging tasks when trying to bring exposure to the problem. Often, pastors and religious leaders will debate and discredit the few who answer the call to bring enlightenment to the blatant misinterpretation of the Bible. They call it the prosperity gospel and call the crusaders "money hungry," "greedy," and more. A lot of pastors or leaders who have an understanding that God wants to prosper His people would not publicly address the topic of prosperity for fear of attack and scrutiny. So to the crusaders who have a mantle to teach as many people who would listen to what the word of God has to say about His blessings, the task is heavy along a road lined with attacks and discouragement.

As part of the covenant of peace, God has taken it upon Himself to break the curse of slavery from over His people. He is setting people free from false beliefs that have contaminated their minds by teaching He is a mean God or that we have to live in lack and suffer; if we disobey Him we are all going to hell. God is using men and women on this earth during this present time, to teach and demonstrate that He wants each of us to live a complete life. He is setting us free from the slavery that has held our minds in captivity believing that we must always sacrifice and never receive a reward for it. We are becoming liberated from thinking that life is supposed to be hard and only the strong survive. From living in survival mode to conquering the world for Christ, God is setting people free from the spirit of oppression, depression and generational curses that have engrained its stain of poverty on the minds and hearts of His people.

Religious leaders, who hold their followers captive to the anti-prosperity belief system without trying to explore and learn what the word of God really says, will be accountable to God for their flock. God has already made a promise to rescue the enslaved from their slave masters.

Chapter Five

Rewards of the Covenant of Peace

We have looked at the components of the covenant in terms of what God promises to do for us. Now let us look at what the benefits will be for those who enter into this promise with God.

LIVE IN SAFETY

With Jesus Christ, the Son of God, as your shepherd you can expect to live a life that is fully protected from anything that can happen in the physical and spiritual world. This does not mean that you will never be threatened with danger. It does not suggest that situations and circumstances will not arise to threaten your existence on this earth. What it denotes is while these threats may occur; your shepherd will drive them away. There will be times when you may be fully aware of the threat or impending danger. You may feel the taxing effects of it, nevertheless the promise God has made is that you will camp safely in the wildest places and sleep in the woods without fear. You will be able to live on a daily basis without fear because you have a confidence that God through His Son Jesus Christ will fight every battle on every side just for you. He will not allow anyone to come into your territory and destroy you. Proverbs 16:7 states, "When people's lives please the Lord, even their enemies are at peace with them." Solomon wrote this knowing his life was a clear example of this truth. He was a king for many years and never went to war.

No Longer Be Prey For Other Nations

In the animal kingdom, it is required that each animal be strong and alert in order to survive in the jungle. Often the weak, sick, lame and babes who have not had a chance to fully develop fall prey to the bigger, stronger animals around them. Through no fault of their own, they become victims in an environment that requires a certain level of performance. What's interesting is that the hunter can sense or smell those who are the weaker ones. Sometimes when it's not clear where the weaker or injured ones are, they spread fear and mayhem, causing all the animals to panic and scatter. Those who fall behind often become prey for the hunter. In their weakened, injured or inexperienced state, they are defenseless against the hunter. The end result is inevitable.

As I watch many of the nature programs, I find myself routing for the prey hoping that by some miracle it would get away and not become dinner for the hunter. And, sometimes by a twist of fate, the prey escapes.

In the world we live in, many people are prey and others are predators. We often become prey to the giant predators that surround us through displays of weakness in areas of our lives. A weakness is any area in which you are not strong or knowledgeable; any area in which you are not fully equipped to deal with the situations and circumstances that you face on a daily basis. These areas of weakness can manifest in education, finances, psychological, and physical forms. For example, you have only a grade school education, but have to make financial decisions that are presented to you at college level or even higher. In order for you to fully understand and benefit in this financial situation, you will have to seek out the assistance of someone who is more experienced in this field than you. You then rely on the knowledge of this person and have to put a certain level of confidence in them in order for you to make sound, informed decisions. Since you are in a position of weakness, you're now forced to depend on someone else to operate with integrity. You are relying on them to be honest and care enough to protect your interest. Should you receive this assistance from a predator who now knows your weakness, you may become prey. This predator can now use your weakness against you and exploit your finances for their personal gain. It happens daily.

God is saying that in His covenant of peace, you will no longer be prey. He will position you with the right people in every circumstance. Despite your areas of weakness, God will ensure that you are surrounded with people who will be a source of strength to you. These people will watch over and protect your investment. God will give you wisdom to identify men and women of integrity who will fill the gaps in every area of weakness in your life. In business we would call this staffing your weakness.

One area of weakness I had in business was that I realized as a black business owner who was excessively overweight, I was not the best choice for front line representation of the company I was trying to build. I assessed my professional environment and realized that the world in which I wanted to do business was not prepared to receive this morbidly obese black woman as a serious entrepreneur in a profession where it was highly probable that no black person had started this type of business before. I knew I was capable of doing what God had placed in my heart. I was educated and fully trained in the area but professionally people were not taking me serious. They didn't view me as capable of attaining the goal I'd set for myself. I decided that if they were not going to meet me at the level I knew I was at, then I was going to give them what they understood. So, I hired a face. I hired someone who they would receive without question and operated in my strength as the entrepreneur who wanted to build a successful business. I was able to do my job of building a highly successful company without the pressure of trying to prove myself as worthy to people who were bound by their own prejudices.

I've often been asked how it made me feel to have people unwilling to do business with me either because of my race, gender or other physical characteristics. In retrospect, the hardest part of the situation was that I didn't know why I wasn't procuring business. Once I realized what the problem was I made the decision to do something about it. Determinedly, I placed my focus on the solution to my problem. I spent little time thinking or wallowing in self-pity as to life's injustices and sought after God for His wisdom on how to handle the matter. I refused to squander my time attempting to change people's perception of me. Instead, I invested my energy into fixing it by hiring someone who society perceived at face value as the ideal image of success.

This person represented my company for business development purposes and allowed me to focus on what I discerned would be my best contribution. It wasn't my problem that others didn't see my value. However, it was imperative that I knew and accepted my value. Allowing someone else to be the face of my company did not deduct from my self-esteem in the least bit because I knew the truth, which lived inside of me. That truth was that I could do all things through Christ who strengthens me. I didn't feel the need to be seen nor heard as the sole owner of my business, but I felt it necessary to build and maintain what God was doing in my life. I believed there would be plenty of time to deal with the issues of society but it wasn't the time for me to fight the cause. God did not allow me to remain prey.

No Longer Be Devoured By Wild Animals

Even when you're in the midst of a crisis, God is keeping His covenant. When you believe that you are about to be consumed by the situation or circumstance you happen to find yourself in, He provides a way to escape. He provides a way in which you can avoid being devoured.

In the covenant of peace, not only will God preclude you from becoming prey, you will not be taken advantage of by the people who circulate in and out of your life. He didn't say the wild animals wouldn't come near you or enter your territory. But He does promise that you will not be prey (devoured or destroyed). And, if you aren't viewed as prey by the wild animals around you, there is no fear of being eaten. After all, a predator only attacks what it perceives as food. You can swim with the sharks and not be consumed. You can still win!

What does this really mean? It means that God will give you revelation, relationships, strategies and resources that will allow you to effectively navigate the channels of your life. These gifts from God will allow you to identify the enemy and implement strategies that will allow you to complete this journey of your life having fulfilled your dreams, visions and purpose. For some, this will be fulfilling your destiny of having reached self-actualization.

Never Again Suffer From Famines

Psalms 37:25 states that the people in right standing with God will never be forsaken nor will their children beg for bread. God promises to ensure that we never experience lack in our households, businesses, etc. To experience famine, does not only pertain to food. It includes any area of your life in which you experience deprivation. Yes, you may not have food, but additionally it means that there is a root cause for the lack of food. For some, the problem may be cash flow and they simply don't have enough money to buy food. However, on a deeper level, there is another problem that led to the decrease or lack of finances. Examining the source of your finances will help determine the problem or cause of the deficit. Understanding what caused that source to dry up and how to regenerate the funds that make it possible for you to buy food is a part of the solution.

Deprivation in love, health and relationships are areas in which people can experience famine. Anywhere this is an imbalance in your life, it will show up as excess or lack.

A popular scripture Christians love to quote is that the wealth of the wicked is laid up for the righteous. Some believe that a wealthy individual will die and leave them an inheritance. Others believe that by some supernatural act of God, He is going to take away all that another person has worked hard for and give it to them because they are the righteous. Some trust that if they're servants of God or ministers of the gospel, then it's the responsibility of other people to take care of them. I believe that wealth transfers from one person to the other when there is an exchange of goods and services. I will receive wealth when I provide the goods and services needed by the wealth holder. This wealth holder may or may not be a "wicked" person but because of the excessive abundance that God has blessed my field with, I can now exchange it for increase in other areas of my life; hence a transfer of the wealth of the world to the righteous or to the one who is in right standing with God.

God brings the blessing of increase into our lives but it still remains our responsibility to make what God gives us work in a manner that we never experience famine. Many blame lack or seasons of famine in their lives on a test from God or the attack of the enemy. The actual truth for most is that we've made wrong choices with what God provided for us. We received the bumper crop. The anointing of increase and favor came upon our lives but somehow we made choices that caused an exit of blessings rather than an increase. So now we are living with the consequences of our decisions. It will take repentance and obedience to God to repair and restore the covenant of peace.

Under the covenant of peace, God promises to ensure that we never again suffer from famine. The works of our hands will prosper. Increase will be all around us and even within our homes. Our businesses, investments, children and other relatives will be blessed with abundance. For those who are employed, you will increase in promotions, salary and favor.

Never Again Suffer From Insults of Foreign Nations

One of the most amazing experiences Christians have is ridicule from people who denigrate their beliefs and customs. A lot of Christians have had a hard time convincing non-believers to accept and follow the principles of the Bible. One of the main reasons people have rejected the church and its teachings is because, there has been little proof that believing in God or His son Jesus Christ is worthwhile. A huge percentage of Christians are poor, under educated and fail to see the world from a global perspective. To accept and serve this God implies a life of deprivation and void of pleasure. The rules and restrictions placed by religious sectors makes serving God burdensome more than rewarding. People just can't understand or accept a god who would require that people live in poverty, sickness and oppression. If He is the god that you say He is then why aren't you in a better position than me? Why should I give up the success that I am experiencing for a god that may require that I give it all away and live in misery?

Most Christians do not understand their faith. Most cannot answer the basic questions of a non-believer who is seeking answers in this complex world. As a result, many nations and religions have come to look down on Christians as weak, poor and floundering. There is little respect for Christians as world changers because we have not taken the time to master an understanding of what the word of God says. Therefore, we are unprepared to discuss little beyond salvation and physical healing. Because we have only embraced certain aspects of the word of God, we are ill equipped to deal with the waterfall of questions, accusations and persecutions from a society that is growing more and more away from God. It would appear as though we are powerless.

In the covenant of peace, God is promising that we will no longer be ridiculed by foreign nations or religions. Within the United States alone you can find people from practically every nation and nearly every religion in the world. All have the freedom to worship the god of their choice and are free to believe whatever they perceive is right for them. Yet, with all of this freedom to worship, Christians are struggling to grow in the foundations of their faith in America. More people are turning to other religions than to Christianity. Society scoffs at the person who promotes the name of Jesus unless they limit their messages to inspirations. If it's not a message that says God loves everyone, you can be anything you want to be, your future can be brighter with a positive mental attitude, etc., they don't want to hear or accept the message. After all, who wants to serve a god that condemns us to hell for our sins, causes sickness and disease to affect people, allows our children to be raped and murdered, takes away our money and sucks the joy out of life? To want to be a part of this god is ridiculous and borderline insane. Those who choose such a life are just the same.

As God blesses us under the covenant of peace, our lives become balanced. We have to develop a strong foundation of an understanding of whom and what God really is. We prosper in health, education and in our emotional beings. Evidence of this balance to the world is an increase in our prosperity. We prosper financially through either our professions or through the daily operations of businesses. God envelops every aspect of our lives and causes it to produce at a level that all foreign nations must recognize and respect that we are the blessed of the Lord. Instead of insults, there is respect for what God has done in our lives. An example of this is the Jewish religion. They are the wealthiest of all religious groups and have managed to dominate the list of the wealthiest people in America. Because of the blessing of financial increase that has manifested in their lives, most people respect their influence and power. While many may not agree with their religious beliefs or practices, there is a respect and emulation of their financial habits in order for others to experience this same financial increase in their lives.

God wants to do the same thing for us as the heirs or descendants of Abraham. Under the Abrahamic covenant, God promises to set us high above all the nations of the earth; bless our children, crops, animals, fruit and bread baskets; bless us everywhere we go and in whatever we do. God guarantees a blessing on everything we do and to fill our storehouses with grain; God promises to give us prosperity and send the rain at the proper time in order to bless all the work of our hands; God promises that we will be the head and not the tail, we will be on the top and never at the bottom; God promises that we will lend to many and not borrow; God also promises that all nations of the world will know that we are a people claimed by God (Deuteronomy 28:1-14).

Just as Jews are respected for their financial influence, so are Christians to walk in the same anointing for prosperity. Paul outlines the connection between the blessings of Abraham and those who chose to believe in God. In Galatians 3:7-9 and 14, Paul wrote:

"The real children of Abraham, then, are those who put their faith in God."

"What's more the Scriptures looked forward to this time when God would declare the Gentiles to be righteous because of their faith." God proclaimed this good news to Abraham long ago when he said, "All nations will be blessed through you."

"So all who put their faith in Christ share the same blessing Abraham received because of his faith."

"Through Christ Jesus, God has blessed the Gentiles with the same blessing he promised to Abraham, so that we who are believers might receive the promised Holy Spirit through faith."

We serve a God who loves us so much He established covenants which cannot be broken to ensure we are always blessed and prosperous.

BE FAMOUS FOR YOUR CROPS

In previous elements of the covenant, God promises that He will send the showers to water our crop at the appropriate times and cause our fields and orchards to produce a bumper crop. This is the evidence of all the hard work that is put into ensuring God has something to bless when He implements multiplication in our lives. For some people the field or orchard may be a start-up business, expansion of an existing business, completion of a college degree and pursuing a career, nurturing a family, pursuing ministry. Whatever the crop, it requires that each of us take some form of action so that when the showers begin to fall, our seeds are in the right place. It is time to receive the increase that God promises for our lives. He promises to bless the works of our hands.

When I began my career in the medical field, I never dreamed of owning my own business. Later, I became more despondent after moving to America realizing that because of my outward appearance, society had already developed a category into which I was expected to fit. Having dumped the self-pity mentality, I began to explore and learn my new environment, the country that has now become my home. I empowered myself by taking classes on understanding diverse cultures and religions in addition to, how a person's belief system shaped their behaviors. In essence, I invested in socializing within my environment. Having grasped a fundamental understanding of what people thought of me, and the categories they felt I should adapt to, I made a conscious decision to explore my differences. Yes, I was a heavy black, immigrant woman but I believed I could accomplish anything I desired once I determined it was what I aspired to achieve.

At the time I created my company in the pharmaceutical research arena in 2001, the racial makeup of professionals in this area was predominantly Caucasian with a minuscule amount of Blacks, Hispanics and others. I've traveled to meetings all over the world and have been the only black person in a room of 300 to 500 medical professionals. To the person who lacks confidence, this can be intimidating but I decided to use this to my advantage. First of all, I knew that upon meeting me, all of these scientists and executives from various pharmaceutical companies would never forget me because I stood out. Besides, it was difficult to miss me in any room. To top it all off, I had a pleasant and cheerful attitude to go with a brain that understood my industry. When I made a business development phone call to these people, they remembered me and were more likely to do business with me than not because God used my difference to allow them to remember and gave me favor with them.

There was another key element that worked in my favor. The federal government issued a report stating pharmaceutical companies needed to include more minority subjects in the research of their newly developed drugs. It was necessary in order to ensure safety and effectiveness across all racial groups. This would have to be done for all new drugs in development in order for them to be considered for market approval. Well, what do you know? My company, which I believe was one of the first black owned pharmaceutical research companies, was able to provide this service. After all, we were predominantly minorities (Blacks and Hispanics) and we had a relationship in communities that could never be effectively penetrated by Caucasians because of lack of familiarity.

It was exceptionally challenging to penetrate African-American communities due to the previous history of abuse in research such as the Tuskegee experiment. Pharmaceutical companies were aware that in order to include minorities in clinical drug trials, it would require a certain level of trust and access. And there was this woman who stood out at every meeting. What was her name again? What was the name of the company she worked? Do you think she can reach these target groups for us? Before long, my research company was busy filling the demand for more research across ethnic and racial lines. We trained as many minorities as we could to fill the roles of principal investigators (doctors who specialize in clinical drug trials), research coordinators and assistants. In addition, I was invited to consult on the development of computer software that would decrease time and the volume of paper utilized in research by one of the largest pharmaceutical companies in America. I was able to travel the world first class and live in some of the best hotels one can imagine, paid for by the scope of my work. Another way to look at it is that everything favorable stemmed from the seeds I had planted.

God used the seeds I'd already planted by multiplying and increasing the grounds that I prepared. I educated myself, evaluated the soil in which I was going to plant my seeds and invested in making sure that whenever the rains began to fall, my field would produce the best harvest.

Understanding that only God could have caused my business to prosper, it was my responsibility to choose daily to prepare the grounds of my life for the increase that could only come from God. And He did just what He said He would do. We became the "go to" company for minority subjects and we prospered abundantly.

I am certain there were many instances in which my judgment was questioned because of my race, gender, physical characteristics, immigration status or whatever the choice of doubt was. Nevertheless, I refused to waste my valuable time acknowledging or allowing it to detract from what God was doing in my life. I concentrated on each area of my life and made changes or adjustments to my seeds and soil as the forecasted needs arose.

Eventually, I lost most of my extra weight for health reasons. I never allowed it to become a crutch or excuse to pass blame for my lack of accomplishment. I took the time to recognize my strengths and weaknesses and discovered ways in which each could help me progress to my destiny. Initially my race was a hindrance but God used it as a seed to produce a bountiful harvest in my life. Your difference or uniqueness is a seed that God can use to catapult you into the life you desire to live. It first requires that you recognize and embrace it rather than deny or question God on why He made you a certain way. It is a seed, which you must plant in the appropriate field in order to give God the opportunity to increase or prosper you.

Know That He Is Your God And He Is With You

What brought me to the United States was my difference and a need for that difference to be cultivated. It gave me the ability to thrive. I was a licensed registered nurse in The Bahamas when God instructed me to move to the United States to pursue higher education. At the time, I was the single mother of a two-year-old son. I didn't have any financial resources available and I was unsure of how it was going to be possible but I remained obedient to God. Then one day at work a colleague handed me an application for the Florida State Board exam for Registered Nurses. There was a shortage of registered nurses and if I passed the exam, I could become licensed and work in the United States. Immediately, I recognized that God was opening a door for me to pursue the advanced education He had spoken to me about. I took the exam and was hired by one of South Florida's largest hospitals. Within eight months of receiving an instruction from the Lord, I moved to Florida with a job and a work visa obtained through the hospital that hired me. God blessed me in such a way that before I even left my country, I had permission for my son and I to live and work in the USA.

Without having supplementary financial support I refused to give up and worked hard. God gave me instructions in the bedroom of my apartment in Nassau and I was relentless in following them. I worked two, sometimes three jobs and paid cash for a Bachelor's and Master's degree in science. I excelled in my field and received numerous promotions within the institution I worked for. I prayed, asking God for His guidance in my decisions and became a Director of one of the most successful joint research ventures in South Florida between Mount Sinai Medical Center and the University of Miami. Wow, what a faithful God! I thought this was the pinnacle of my success and really didn't want to reach further.

In a chain of events, that I truly believe only God could have orchestrated, I ended up starting my own research company without any money. I was the only employee and I couldn't even pay myself. I had to reach deep inside of my faith in God and believe without a doubt that I was in His will and He would not allow me to fail. All this faith didn't stop my hair from falling out or eliminate the stress but I believed God. Each morning, drained of energy, I rolled out of bed onto my knees. The only words I could find to say were, "God, I trust you to provide for me today," then I'd go about the task of trying to find business for my company.

My first contract dealt with Alzheimer's disease in patients who resided in nursing homes. At the time, there wasn't an effective treatment or cure for Alzheimer's disease. Many families were desperate for answers. I gained access to the nursing homes through the administration but still required family members to agree to the use of the experimental medication for their loved ones. I was excited. I had a contract, a nursing home that agreed to the research program and family members who were open to the idea of using an experimental medication to improve the memory of their loved ones. I was on top of the world.

In one of the greatest tests of my faith in God, the very first two patients whose families signed the consent for their relative to participate, passed away. It happened before I could commence my evaluations to qualify them for the program. Neither of the deaths had anything to do with the research. Sadly, one broke a hip and died of a fat embolus and the other passed quietly in her sleep. To compound matters even further, the son of one of the patients died of a heart attack the night after he signed the consent and the patient (his mother) died within 24 hours of him. I was devastated for the families. How could this be? Am I truly in the will of God?

My bank account was empty. My contract was based on performance and I had not earned a penny as of yet. The administrator at the nursing home jokingly mentioned the coincidences and encouraged me to keep trying. I went home and cried out before God because He knew my heart, intention and destiny. That was the last time I ever had a patient die in the 12 years of my company.

Gradually, business began to increase. Within five months of operations, the tragic events of September 11, 2001 occurred. I recall arriving at the nursing home with a representative of a pharmaceutical company. Together, we watched the events tragically unfold on television. She had just arrived from outside of New York City and was desperate to reach her husband. The chaos was immeasurable. Then something amazing happened that afternoon. My cell phone rang. It was the manager of the project I was working on. She commented on the attacks and went on to tell me that she was pleased with my work. Because of this, the team decided to increase my contracted budget by six figures and provided a budget so I could hire an assistant in order to complete the contract faster. At the end of the contract I would receive a bonus. If it had been under any other circumstances, I would've jumped up and down screaming while praising God. But on that day, I couldn't, because of the devastation, loss of tremendous life and the ongoing situation that was unfolding with the terrorist attacks. It weighed heavily on my heart. So I locked myself in an empty room at the nursing home and praised God in my own way.

God proved to me that He was my God and that He was with me daily. He never left me even when it seemed the odds were stacked against me. He guided me to the right decisions, made sure all of my expenses were paid and never allowed my son and I to go hungry. I learned that He is my God in every area of my life. By following His instructions, I learned never to beg or ask a person to meet my needs. If God is my provider, my Jehovah-Jireh, then to ask anyone else to supply my needs meant I was replacing Him as my God. I was really telling God that I trusted the person for their ability to provide for me more than I trusted Him. After all that God had brought me through there was no way I could put that level of faith or confidence in any human being.

God is our God. He loves us so much He established a covenant of peace to ensure that we always have access to His abundant blessings. He wants to do miraculous things for each of us who would trust Him every day of our lives. All we have to do is apply the principals required for the blessings and trust Him to deliver the harvest.

Chapter Six

Terms of the Covenant

When you review all that God has said so far about the covenant of peace, you must now begin to realize that if you are to receive all that God has for you, there are actions required of you. You are probably wondering what can I do to experience the covenant of peace in my life? Some of you want to be all that God has called you to be while others just want a life of peace and contentment in God.

TERM #1:
TRUST IN GOD
TO PROTECT AND KEEP YOU

God refers to us as His sheep. It is known that sheep are not defensive animals. They are usually vulnerable and require protection because they were not created with methods to defend themselves. A shepherd or sheepherder is necessary to protect these animals at all times from predators who want to devour them. Apostle Peter cautions in 1 Peter 5:8 to stay alert because the enemy (the devil) prowls around like a roaring lion looking for someone to devour. That includes anything or anyone he and his companions come across. In Ephesians 6:12, Paul let us know that our fight is not with flesh and blood enemies but against evil and wickedness that we cannot see. He then encourages us in Ephesians 6:13-17 to put on God's armor so we may be able to overcome and resist the attacks that come against us. He gives a definite insight that you are engaged in a battle.

Each piece of God's armor has a significant defense mechanism to protect in battle. The helmet of salvation covers the head. It protects our knowledge, ability to think, reasoning and ability to determine right from wrong. It is the center of our logic. It protects our knowledge of our salvation and what we see and hear.

The breastplate of righteousness protects the heart, which is a vital organ for the sustaining of life. The Bible encourages us to guard our heart because from it we make decisions concerning our lives. Wearing the breastplate of righteousness means that your right standing with God is fully protected. What does not enter your head through the helmet of salvation cannot enter your heart.

The loin is the very center of our reproductive ability. Having our loins girded with truth ensures that the truth of God's word, which we are responsible to carry into the world, is protected. From the loins we produce the future. So from a loin of truth, we will reproduce the perpetual truth of God's word and goodness.

The shield of faith offers protection from anything the enemy throws at us. It deflects arrows and the fiery darts of the enemy. What's interesting about the shield of faith is that this is a defense of war that requires that we take hold of it. It's a piece of the armor that we have to choose to pick up and choose when and how to hold it to protect us. If we don't hold it correctly, it will not work. The Bible says, if you have faith as big as a grain of mustard seed, you shall speak to a mountain and it will move. The same applies here. You have to believe that when you hold this shield, it will protect you no matter what you see coming your way. Another significant indication here is that you are holding the shield with hands that God has already blessed to prosper. Having faith means that you do not allow fear, doubt or unbelief to enter with you into battle.

The sword of the spirit is the word of God. You are holding in your hand every promise of the word of God. You are holding as a weapon every word that God has said. You can boldly tell the enemy that he is defeated just as Jesus did when He was tempted. Jesus did not engage in conversation with the devil. He simply said, "It is written." God has now given you the same power to let the enemy know what His written word says.

The one component of the armor that is so very connected to the covenant of peace is having your feet shod with the preparation of the gospel of peace. I meditated on this one for some time asking God for clarity as to what this really meant. I emailed a few ministers of the gospel and asked for insight on what their interpretation of this piece of the armor meant. However, I only received one response. I understood that shod meant to put on shoes but what does "preparation of the gospel of peace" actually mean? To prepare, obviously means that we have to do something in advance but what are we to do in advance? The gospel is the good news of Jesus Christ. So does the gospel of peace mean to prepare ourselves with the knowledge of knowing that Jesus Christ came as the Savior of the world and He wants us to win souls and live in harmony with others? If God is telling us to put on armor because we are in a battle, why then would we try to be in harmony with our attacker? The mere fact that we have to put on armor signifies that the battle has already begun and all negotiations of peace and harmony have failed. The enemy is on the attack and we have been summoned to fight.

The "peace" in the covenant of peace and the gospel of peace are both representative of the same. In the covenant of peace, God promises that we will live without fear, lack or ridicule. He promises that we, along with our entire household, will be blessed in a bountiful way. We are whole spiritually, physically, psychologically and especially financially. There is nothing missing, lacking or broken in our lives. The gospel of peace now means that we have been prepared not only with the message of Jesus Christ but we are fully equipped to carry that message into battle to destroy the plans and attacks of the enemy. There is nothing to hinder us. We have health, strength, strong bonds of love through family, friends and relatives, strategic connections and relationships. Most importantly, we have the financial resources to take the gospel of Jesus Christ to the ends of the earth.

The feet represent our mobility, territory and dominion. In Deuteronomy 11:24 when God blessed Abraham, He told him that "Wherever you set foot, that land will be yours..." This was a promise to return the dominion man lost when Adam disobeyed God in the Garden of Eden. Having promised Abraham that everywhere he placed his feet he would own it, the pierced feet of Jesus then becomes significant of the return of our dominion and right to regain territory. We are no longer disinherited children of the King. We have the right to take charge in every environment we find ourselves in. God returned our rights through the shedding of Jesus' blood as they nailed His feet to the cross. Not only do we have the protected resources but we now have the power to enter into battle knowing that we are fully able to conquer territory lost to the enemy.

The armor of God is only as effective as the weakest part. Most Christians are sure of their salvation; they are in right standing with God. They know and understand the truth of God's word. Their faith, in the word of God that they understand, is unwavering. But the gospel of peace is where they are weak. They are so distracted either by worries and fears concerning their lives and provisions that they are too weak to fight. Lack of health, education, emotional imbalances, unstable family life, unhealthy relationships and alliances along with rising debt has handicapped them in the preparation for battle. The enemy has managed to weaken their defenses by suppressing finances and silencing their voices in the decision making process of society. They are worried, burdened with feelings of helplessness and hopelessness as their lives spiral out of control.

Meanwhile, the enemy is not threatened when Christians speak about the armor because he has ripped a hole in their defenses. There is no dominion, power or ability to take back anything he has stolen. We are operating with a form of godliness but have been robbed of the power God has given us.

TERM #2:
RENEW YOUR MIND

In order for the truth of God's word to manifest in your life, you have to open your mind and heart to the possibilities that what I thought I know, I may not really know. You may have to accept that someone, somewhere may have taught you something for which there is no factual basis in the word of God. You may have to face the reality that what I fear is not reality and all of what I thought were my faults and weaknesses are really unique qualities that God wants to use for His glory. You may have to face the reality that you may be your own worst enemy. You may be the one who has sabotaged your own dreams through feelings of insecurity and not knowing who and what you are in Christ. Most importantly, you may have to recognize that God is not a religion. He is a being with whom you can have an experience as well as a relationship. He operates in our lives in ways that we understand and can identify with. He speaks, listens, and is compassionate and loving. He is extremely respectful of the fact that He created us superior to all other animals by giving us the right to choose. The right includes choosing or rejecting Him and His blessings. He allows us to make our choices, suffer the consequences, and only intervenes when we invite Him into our circumstances. You may need to accept and believe that God created every one of us with a plan and a purpose in mind. There is no situation from which He cannot produce a harvest of blessings out of it. To understand these things, you must be willing to humble yourself before God.

The point I am making here is that God has not changed from Genesis to Revelation. The God that created the earth, man, woman and all the animals is the same God who has blessed and protected man over the centuries. He blessed then and He continues to bless us even now. Every promise He ever made in the Bible, which is His constant conversation with us, has always been kept. If God says He will bless you and He wants you to prosper, He means it. He is not a man that He should lie, nor is He the son of man that He has to say He is sorry for saying something in error or for making a promise He can't keep.

The renewing of your mind begins with reading and understanding the word of God for yourself. It is your responsibility to open the word of God and read it. Verify the scriptures that are quoted to you, in this book and from every man or woman of God. Authenticate what the word of God says. You have the right to choose to accept or reject what people are speaking based on verification in the word of God. Don't just accept what people say. Try, test and prove God to be the God of His word. Relying on the philosophy of other people will not only leave you open to *false belief systems* and divert your attention from the true knowledge of God's word, but it will set you up for disappointment.

By the renewing of your focus back to God through His word, you will realize that even the greatest preachers or evangelists are all human and thereby fallible and subject to error. Your liberty is not tied to their success or failure but rather to the promises of God. He was, is and will be forever, the same.

Some teachers of the Bible would probably question how could the covenant of peace be a true covenant when there is no shedding of blood? Most biblical covenants are sealed with the shedding of blood. This is where Jesus Christ comes in. He is the Shepherd God sent into this world to redeem man from all past curses and judgments. Through the shedding of His blood, the curse of poverty was broken from over our lives.

My goal is not to teach you a new way but to awaken what is already inside of you. You were born with all that you need to be what God has called you to be. Remember, in Jeremiah 1, God told Jeremiah that He knew him before he was even conceived in his mother's womb. That He had already set him apart to be a prophet to the nations. God created all of us with the finished product in mind. It is up to us to identify and develop what is in us. My talents are unique to me and yours are unique to you.

Begin the journey of renewing your mind by coming to terms with the areas of your life where change is needed. Seek help from whomever is qualified to help you. Work on fixing yourself first by reading the word of God daily. Develop healthy habits and maintain them daily so they go with you into a prosperous future. These habits will build a strong moral and ethical character.

Identify your passion and pursue ways to succeed in that area so you can serve people to the best of your abilities. A way to identify your passion is to identify what moves you in a positive and negative way. What makes you feel good? What makes you feel angry? What makes you feel pain?

I experience great pleasure in seeing people have their dreams come true. On the other hand, I experience pain when observing poverty. It is deeply distressing to the point of anger when I see people using the name of God to exploit others for their personal gain. Christians have lost credibility because of it and it makes me feel like I have to do something. So I recognized that part of my purpose during my time here on earth is to teach people how to prosper, be an example of integrity in business and ministry while teaching others, through the word of God, how to identify when situations and circumstances are not of God.

In order for the chains of slavery to be broken from over our lives, we have to first recognize that we have been enslaved in so many ways to wrong ideas and opinions. Society has categorized and pigeonholed us into being a certain kind of way based on race, gender, ethnicity, religion, country of origin, familial relations and the list goes on and on. Some of us have accepted the stereotypes and have allowed ourselves to fall in line with what society says we are to be. God says we are created in His image. Which means everyone one of us looks like God regardless of where and whom we come from. Being unwilling to accept someone because of his or her differences is a bold in your face confrontation with God, letting Him know that He made a mistake that offends you. The funny thing here is that the only person who really cares what you think is you. God knows His plan for each person and will not change it because it offends you. The only person, who has the power to change the outcome of their life, is the one who buys into the false belief that there is something wrong with the way they were created. They are allowing the opinions of others to drive their decisions. God wants you to be free from the opinions of man and focus on the fact that you were wonderfully and fearfully made in His image and that's all you need to know.

It is believed that our earliest memories of money and its significance to life usually shapes the way in which we handle our finances for the rest of our lives unless something later changes that perception. As I was growing up, I learned through my mother that hard work was how you made money. From approximately seven-years-old, I helped her prepare her food to sell as a lunch vendor at the primary school. My mother would pack the food into a grocery cart and walk three miles each way twice a day to sell lunch to the school children. Some did not have money so she often gave away the food. At the end of the day my mother would have made an average of twenty-dollars and she was happy. Later in life, as a business owner, I worked long hours and my company was successful. However, one day I divided the number of hours I was working into the amount of money I was paying myself and discovered that I was the lowest paid person in my company. What I had learned from my mother was how to work hard for very little money. I didn't know how to get paid for what I was worth. At that point, I realized it was essential to change my thinking and my approach.

TERM #3:
SOW SEED DAILY

In the book of Ecclesiastes 11:6 we are encouraged to "Plant your seed in the morning and keep busy all afternoon, for you don't know if profit will come to one activity or another—or maybe both."

Recognizing that only God will give us the rain at the right time to ensure a proper harvest, we must also realize that God requires something from us. If we didn't plant seeds, regardless of when and how the rain falls, there won't be any harvest because we failed to do our part. Can we blame God for the lack of produce in our lives when He has already told you He will send the rain in due season? To blame the lack of resources and finances in our lives on the will of God should be considered blasphemous because for every time we do our due diligence, God has an obligation under the covenant of peace to bless. Remember, we have already established that God is not a man that he would lie or change His mind. He will do what He says He will do. There is no mention anywhere in the Bible that God ever planted a field for anyone but He did say He will protect that seed and ensure it produces a harvest.

"Those too lazy to plow in the right season will have no food at the harvest" (Proverbs 20:4).

In Luke 10:2, it tells us to pray to the Lord of the harvest which is God. God controls the rain and He controls the harvest based on what you've planted.

I cannot stress to you enough that God is Lord of the harvest. I first heard this from the late Dr. Oral Roberts in a television interview in the last years of his life. At the time, I knew very little on the practice of seedtime and harvest so what he was saying was intriguing to me. As I listened intently, a few things stuck with me.

1) One should sow a seed to produce the harvest you want.
2) When in need you can cash in a seed for a desired harvest.
3) Jesus is Lord of the harvest.

He went on to explain each and from then I began to explore, "Jesus is Lord of the harvest." What I discovered was that in order for God to give me a harvest, I had to first plant a seed. The Bible tells us to plant in the morning and in the evening because we don't know which will produce a harvest. I'd been planting seeds into ministries and the lives of people for many years but I never quite grasped the concept that if I sowed a seed, I should expect to receive a harvest. After all, a farmer wouldn't plant a field of corn if he didn't expect it to produce enough to have made it worth the effort.

It took much education through other teachers on the topic of prosperity to get me to a level of understanding that if a seed is planted it is supposed to produce a harvest. I had mastered the art of giving or sowing into other people, but I couldn't grasp that God wanted me to receive just as those people received from me. In a time of introspection, I realized that more than half of the time, I gave out of a sense of obligation rather than from a place of joy in knowing that I was making a difference in people's lives or that my Heavenly Father wanted to increase me. After years of giving and receiving very little in return, the fun in giving had dissipated. I had conquered greed through my faith to sow but failed to maintain faith for a harvest.

In the book of Malachi 3:10-17 it says that we are to trust God by bringing our tithes and offerings into the house of God. God promises that if we do this, He will open the windows of heaven and pour out such an amazing blessing we will not have adequate room to receive. He also promises to protect our harvest causing it to be bountiful at the right time and without loss. This is directly linked to the covenant of peace, which has similar promises.

At this point some of you may be saying this is just another book to encourage people to give their money to the church. You may even feel discouraged because like me, you have given so much of yourself and have seen little to no harvest for your investment. But, I encourage you to read further. One of the main purposes of this book is to teach you that sowing of seed is not just financial, it incorporates all of you.

When God created you, everything about you is a seed to be sown into this world. Before each of us were formed in the wombs of our mothers, God had already set us apart to complete at least one assignment during our lifetime. The greater the assignment the greater the season of preparation will be. In Jeremiah 29:11 God tells us that He has a plan for each one of us, which includes our prosperity. So each of us is an accumulation of the agenda of God. What is needed is that we begin to sow ourselves, all of us, into the plan and intent of God. Rather than trying to find the parts of the word of God that applies to our lives, we now need to apply our lives to the word of God. This means we should know what the word of God says and allow that word to change who we are. We then conform to the ways in which God intends for us to live.

The most popular categories of summing up your seed sowing is to sow your time, talent and treasure into the house of God. If everything about you is a seed, that means your thoughts, opinions, words, energy, as well as your finances are all seeds that can be sown into the lives of others. Sowing seed is not just about giving to the church. Taking the time to listen and speak kindly to a person is a seed. A hug, a non-judgmental place of refuge for a person who is hurting is a seed. Telling someone they are beautiful in the eyes of God is a seed. And yes, feeding and clothing the poor are all seeds. There is a unique quality in all of us that has the ability to be life changing for a few or many. The goal is to sow all of you and allow God to produce a harvest on your investment.

You are also required to sow into yourself. Don't get so busy taking care of the world that you neglect yourself. It's your responsibility to sow seeds into yourself so God can produce a harvest within and for you. This will empower you to remain inspired about what you do. You will see the rewards of your labor. Spending time reading the word of God, meditating on it and allow God to increase your wisdom, knowledge and understanding are part of your investment into your future development. However, it's your responsibility to seek education, careers, businesses, inventions, acquisition of real estate, relationships with people, mentorship and strategic connections. These are part of plowing and planting the field for God to send the rains and shower down the blessings upon your life. You aren't safe in an environment that you don't own such as your home or the land you plan to invest in. You are subjected to the terms and conditions of the owner or the lender. You must diligently invest to acquire ownership of your environment. Take time to invest in understanding your area of expertise inside and out. Become proficient in what you do and do it at the highest level of excellence. There's always someone watching you. Develop a reputation of integrity. Say what you mean and mean what you say. Meaning, don't make promises you cannot or don't intend to keep. Personally, I prefer to under promise and over deliver. An example would be a client asking me to do something for them within six months. I would only say yes to the six-month period if I knew I could do it in less than that. If I believe it would take longer, I make sure the client understand that their expectation may not be actualized should we move forward. Should the client agree; I'd move forward having set my own deadline with a date that precedes what the client and I agree upon. This way I can exceed my client's expectations while saving us both time and money.

As I was going through high school, nursing school and eventually college, I constantly remembered a phrase someone said to me. "It is better to be ready for an opportunity and never get one, than to have an opportunity and not be ready." I would often think of what would be worse. Ready but without an opportunity or an opportunity and, not ready. I concluded that I'd have a greater regret if I weren't ready. Now I realize that if I prepare for the opportunity, under the covenant of peace, God will give me a reward for my preparation. After all, He is Lord of the harvest. My years of reading, seeking advanced education, sowing kindness, favor and finances into the lives of other people, are all being rewarded by God on some level or another. I may not always receive the harvest I'm expecting but God always takes care of me.

We have a choice of whether or not we choose to sow seeds. God does not force us to do anything. But His word says if we do our part, He will surely do His. Covenants cannot be broken. He is a covenant keeping God.

Chapter Seven

Moving In 3-D

DESIRE, DETERMINATION AND DISCIPLINE

After completing my master's degree, I began to question God on the direction He wanted my life to go. I felt I'd achieved some measure of success and wanted to start the journey towards self-actualization. In my quiet time with the Lord, the Holy Spirit revealed an understanding that influential and successful people possess three unique character qualities: desire, determination and discipline. I call it the 3-D principle. These three principles are the driving force behind their success. I have been living and speaking on this very principle for the past 12 years, as I am resolute in its outcome.

The 3-D principle, is an experience that starts with a conscious decision that you want to make a difference with your life through influence, power, wealth, or whatever goal you set. People who have achieved positions of immense power, influence and wealth made a decision to be "somebody" or to "make something of themselves." Their desire to accomplish significantly more is driven by a determination to achieve that place of significance. Because of this desire or passion for significance and the determination to achieve it, this group of people live highly disciplined lives that are focused towards the achieving and maintaining of their goals.

At some stage, the goal was set. This goal is the desire. It becomes the passion that drives them on a mission for achievement. While they will acknowledge that there is the possibility of failure, it is their determination that keeps them going in the midst of adversity and unfavorable circumstances.

Discipline plays a major role in whether or not goals and desires are achieved. In this group of people, their desire, determination and discipline for achievement is unwavering and completely focused. They believe so strongly in their goals that it becomes nearly impossible to change their focus. Their goal becomes a lifestyle. Failure only occurs when there is a loss of focus and a lack of discipline.

Desire

Desire is to deem a thing or circumstance so worthy to attain, it brings about a physical or hormonal response. That response determines the extent to which we deliberately exercise willingness to stretch or reach out in order to achieve it. We become acutely aware of the object and the response that occurs in our bodies. There's a sense of pleasure and satisfaction in knowing the desire is attainable.

The level of physical response is determined by the strength or intensity of the desire.

Desire controls determination and tests discipline. Because your desire for something can be so strong, it tells your mind and body that it can accomplish almost anything. The only deterrent to achieving this desire is discipline. Discipline has to be tamed or developed in order to achieve a desired goal.

It is human nature for our desires to vary throughout the many stages of life. This is directly related to where we find ourselves on the continuum of life. But the scriptures direct us that man's desire should be to serve God. Psalms 27:4 says, "The one thing I ask of the Lord—the thing I seek most—to live in the house of the Lord all the days of my life, delighting in the Lord's perfections and meditating in his Temple." The psalmist expresses his desire to dwell in the presence of the Lord all the days of his life. He recognizes that being in the constant presence of the Lord provides three very important gifts: protection, promotion and power. This is outlined in the scriptures that follow, "For he will conceal me there when troubles come; he will hide me in his sanctuary..." (Psalms 27:5). This is protection. He knows that if he is in the presence of the Lord, he will be hidden from the enemy in a place where he cannot be found. "... He will place me out of reach on a high rock" (Psalms 27:5). Here the psalmist is speaking of promotion. To be placed upon a rock is to be promoted by God to a level at which the enemy cannot affect you. You become steadfast and immovable.

"Then I will hold my head high above my enemies who surround me" (Psalms 27:6). This is a position of power. You become a force to be reckoned with, a person of authority in the midst of your enemies. The psalmist goes on to say, "At his sanctuary I will offer sacrifices with shouts of joy, singing and praising the Lord with music." While he recognizes that there are blessings and happiness in the presence of the Lord, he also acknowledges the need to worship the Lord and offer praises.

As Christians we can live successful, victorious lives by having a true desire for the will and intent of God. Christians are to desire the Lord above all else. We can assume our position of power in the Lord. What God has placed us on this earth to accomplish should be the number one priority in order to have success in every area of our lives. Taking care of God's work allows God to take care of you.

David said in Psalms 73:25, "Whom have I in heaven but you? I desire you more than anything on earth." David was the strong and mighty king that he was because he first acknowledged the awesome power of God and he desired to be pleasing to God. David knew that without God he was nothing special despite him being the king of Israel. So what did David do? He embraced God with his dance, praise, worship, and songs but also with his heart. In return, God blessed David with tremendous success throughout his lifetime and for his generations that came after him.

We are urged in I Peter 2:2-3, "Like newborn babies, you must crave pure spiritual milk so that you will grow into a full experience of salvation. Cry out for this nourishment, now that you have had a taste of the Lord's kindness." It is only through the grace of God that we are here today. It is only through the grace of God that we are who we are. So what is it that is keeping us from receiving all that God has for us during our time here on earth? It is our desire for the things of God and for success in all areas of our lives.

James 4:2–4 states, "You want what you don't have, so you scheme and kill to get it. You are jealous of what others have, but you can't get it, so you fight and wage war to take it away from them. Yet you don't have what you want because you don't ask God for it. And even when you ask, you don't get it because your motives are all wrong ... Don't you realize that friendship with the world makes you an enemy of God?" Making God, His plan and intentions for our lives the object of our desires puts us in a rightful place to receive the blessings of God. We would have sown the seed of the *Word of God* into our spirit, which affirms our faith that with God nothing is impossible (Luke 1:37).

In Proverbs 13:12 Solomon says, "Hope deferred makes the heart sick, but a dream fulfilled is a tree of life." To desire the will of God is to be filled with the very life and essence of God. Solomon eloquently outlines the intimacy of this relationship with God by saying "I am my lover's, and he claims me as his own" (Solomon 7:10). When you belong to God and His desire is towards you, you have found yourself in a place that is infinitely saturated with the blessings of God.

As parents we love our children to the point where we continually want to give them things or do things for them. We try to protect them from danger and catch them when they fall. It's the same with God. His desire is towards us. He wants to give us everything that He has for us according to His word.

He wants to indulge us with His goodness. He wants to protect us and to catch us even when we fall.

To belong to God implies that everything about and in you are the property of the Most High God. There is no "me" anymore. You become one with Christ. The Lord guides your actions, thoughts, and words. Some may consider this to be an impossible task but when you desire after the things of God, you experience a renewing of your mind. This renewing of the mind brings about a change in your spirit, which leads to a change in the physical man. Your heart becomes focused on the things of Christ. Your actions and convictions are guided by the constant presence of the Holy Spirit. The things you used to do are no longer a part of your life. You begin to develop a mindset that if God is not in it, you will derive no pleasure from it. I am what the word of God says I am; I have what the word of God says I have; I can do what the word of God says I can do. I have the mind of Christ because I am my beloveds' and His desire is towards me.

Paul in his writings to the Colossians 1:9 told them that he was continually praying that they would have "... complete knowledge of his will and to give you spiritual wisdom and understanding." Paul goes on to emphasize the importance of their lives being honorable and pleasing to God, producing every kind of good fruit. He encouraged them by saying that as they grow, they will know God better. Paul recognized the need to not only desire the will of God, but to adopt a lifestyle that was productive for the kingdom of God. He stated, that we are to be thankful to God for His blessings. The key blessing in these verses is that we are enabled by God "to share in the inheritance that belongs to his people ..."

(Colossians 1:12). We have been set apart by God to be overwhelmingly blessed because we have an inheritance.

Determination

To have a determination for achieving of all that God has planned and intended for your life is to determine in your heart that you will seek and pursue the gifting or uniqueness that is within you. You will discover your difference and how to use that as a seed to sow so that God can produce a bountiful harvest in your life. Additionally, it means to be deliberately determined in your actions and beliefs.

Determination indicates a definite decision that is steadfast, marked out beforehand and usually an unwavering resolve.

Determination is a faith word for the Christian who is seeking the will and intent of God for their lives. You do not know what God has planned for you nonetheless you prepare the soil for the showers of blessings daily. So hand over the reigns of your life to a God who says in His word that He will never leave or forsake you. Although you may be scared, apprehensive and perhaps a bit skeptical, have faith that as long as the reigns are in the hands of God, you cannot fail. This is faith. This is determination.

Determination is what will keep you when all else fails. Determination is what will drive you when the world and even fellow Christians call you crazy or fanatical. Determination will provide reassurance when the Lord tells you to do something that goes against the very nature and laws of man. Your determination is fed by knowing that obedience to God is better than any worldly gain or praise. Determination is what causes you to choose the road less traveled because you know that your reward is a harvest ordained by God. Take deliberate steps to plant seeds of education, training and relationships until such time as God sends the increase. Your preparation may not make sense to many but when God proves us faithful with little things He promotes us to even bigger things.

Your determination and faith are driven by your faith in God. It is the word that says, "I can," "I will," "I am," "I have," but most importantly it says, "Lord, because I believe."

Paul is a prime example of a man determined to fulfill the will and purpose that God had called him to. In Romans 8:38 he says, "And I am convinced that nothing can ever separate us from God's love. Neither death nor life, neither angels nor demons, neither our fears for today nor our worries about tomorrow – not even the powers of hell can separate us from God's love." Wouldn't it be nice to take out the "us" and personalize this scripture for ourselves? Can we be determined to follow the dreams and visions God has placed inside of us regardless of the circumstances?

Paul was facing death for what he believed and the work he had been called to do. Yet, he remained steadfast in faith and commitment to his God. In I Corinthians 2:2 he wrote, "For I decided that while I was with you I would forget everything except Jesus Christ, the one who was crucified." He further demonstrated his faith and commitment to God when he said, "I have fought the good fight, I have finished the race, and I have remained faithful" (II Timothy 4:7).

Discipline

The mere mention of the word discipline brings back memories of our parents and teachers shaping us into well-organized and behaved children. We regard the word discipline with a bit of resistance because we know that there is a requirement of us to govern ourselves. It requires a heightening of our awareness and implementation of pre-determined rules and guidelines. It is our human nature to want to rebel, to do it our way.

Despite what we feel about the word discipline, what does it really mean? Discipline is to have a soundness of mind that brings about a level of self-control. This does not quite fit with our pre-conceived ideas of discipline. We always see discipline as doing things we don't want to do but in actuality, being disciplined means to have self-control and being of a sound mind. So how does it relate to the 3-D experience with God?

To be disciplined is to be a disciple to that which you desire. When you truly desire something, your thoughts are consumed by it. Your actions are based on your desires but you quickly realize that you need a knowledge base to be effectively focused on your goal. You begin to seek avenues through which to obtain this knowledge. You ask questions, read, watch programs, listen to recordings and take classes. Overall, you do whatever it takes to find out as much as you can about your desire and how to attain it. Somewhere along the way you realize that there are some things you will have to change, give up or add to your life in order to accomplish your desire. What's amazing is that you really don't care about the changes you have to make. You are so passionate about your goal it's all you can think about. Until you get it, you will not be happy. Your belief in your desire is so strong that you prepare yourself for its actualization by developing a mindset through education and physical action that you will achieve your desire. All of this is called following after a dream or desire.

To be a disciple is to follow after a teaching or a belief just as Jesus' disciples followed after him. A disciple is not only a pupil, but also someone who strictly adheres to the rules given by the teacher. In Proverbs 19:8 it says, "To acquire wisdom is to love oneself; people who cherish understanding will prosper."

As I was preparing to open my pharmaceutical research business, I had knowledge of what was required because I worked in the field for some time. However, I made the commitment to study and understand the industry I was about to become a part of. I went to several seminars and conferences, received training on the regulations of the federal government and asked questions of every pharmaceutical representative who came to inspect our offices. I solicited their opinion on certain matters and when I was prepared to launch my own company, I asked some of them if they would consider doing business with me. My first two contracts originated from people I developed relationships with. Because I'd taken time to learn everything I could and demonstrated that knowledge to the representatives, I was able to gain their confidence. They knew that I was knowledgeable and capable of handling a contract worth hundreds of thousands of dollars. I constructed my lifestyle around the things I wanted to accomplish. It was essential for me to sustain a consistent discipline towards exercising my knowledge and patience when dealing with pharmaceutical representatives. It wasn't easy and many times my limits were tested but I persevered.

Discipline is governed by both desire and determination. Your desire creates a determination to achieve a goal but discipline can make or break the end results.

Discipline determines how and when you achieve your goal. It requires a constant subjection to the desire. How badly you want something determines the level of discipline you will have. As Christians living a life of discipline means that we read and study the word of God devotedly. We follow after the teachings in the word and allow the Holy Spirit to guide us daily. It means to live a life of obedience to God and the purpose that He has placed on our lives. Acts of discipline are to daily pursue knowledge of the future you are seeking; implement new ideas and build relationships. These are all preparation for a desired harvest.

In John Chapter 8:31-32, Jesus told the disciples, "You are truly my disciples if you remain faithful to my teachings. And you will know the truth, and the truth will set you free." This freedom represents the ability to be mighty and powerful men and women of

God, living victoriously over life's circumstances through the divine word of God.

A life of discipline means to follow after Christ (Luke 14:27-29, 33). It also means to have a life of prosperity and pleasure based on following the instructions of God as outlined in Job 36:10–12.

For most people, they are content to dream and speak of the visions God has placed in them. They have not developed a passion for achievement, have not set goals and have no decisive action plan to take them into the destiny God has for them. Procrastination has taken a strong hold in their lives and defeat is eminent.

"Good planning and hard work lead to prosperity, but hasty shortcuts lead to poverty" (Proverbs 21:5).

Chapter Eight

Reasons People Don't Prosper

THE BATTLE FOR PROSPERITY

The covenant of peace was established to ensure the opportunity for each person to live a prosperous and productive life. It ensures that all who embrace His principles receive the bountiful blessings He intends for each of us while on this earth. It's comforting to know that we serve a God who concerns Himself with our happiness and comfort in addition to preparing an eternal home that exceeds anything that can be found here on earth.

Knowing that we serve a generous, loving God, what would then hinder our ability to embrace His blessings? It is our mind and what we believe to be the truth of God's word. When new revelatory teaching is introduced, it shakes the core of what we have believed for many years. For some of us we will have to discard what our parents, grandparents, pastors and others that we respect, taught us and allow ourselves to embrace the truth of God's word.

Old schools of thought will be challenged and the battle begins.

The battle for prosperity is in the mind. Wrong thinking, lack of knowledge of who God is and what He can do has been combined with a subcultural belief that money is a bad thing, it will corrupt you, God will give me what he wants me to have, etc. These thoughts only serve to falsely pacify the minds and hearts of people when we fail to accomplish our secret dreams and goals. Proverbs 13:12 says, "Hope deferred makes the heart sick, but a dream fulfilled is a tree of life." We've become sick because we are not living the life God intended for us to live. We're experiencing discontentment in our mind, body and soul. You know within yourself you could be more and you actually want more but fear says, "Wait on God. If God wants you to have it He will give it to you." The word of God says He will bless the works of your hands. The question is, what have your hands been busy doing? Have you given God something to bless or have you rested on the seat of passivity and procrastination blaming God for what is lacking in your life? In reality, you haven't done anything to bring about a blessing in your life. You didn't truly believe that God is able to abundantly exceed everything you can ask or think.

Success in life not only requires faith in God, it requires strategic planning, decisive action and an unwavering resolve. This is where many Christians either didn't get the memo or failed to read it. Are we taught to wait on God or prepare for a move of God?

So how do we tap into the blessings of God and activate the covenant of peace in our lives? We first must recognize the reasons why people are not prospering.

Paralysis Of The Mind

Fear can have such a crippling effect on a person. Some people are fearful of stepping into the unknown. They are afraid to take initiative in certain areas of their lives because they don't understand the circumstance or can't predict or guarantee the outcome. Others are fearful because they're unsure of whether or not what they want to do is right for them so doubt effortlessly seeps in. Is this part of God's plan for my life? How do I know if I'm on the right track? Should I even be pursuing such goals? Others are fearful that being prosperous, which many interpret as being financially secure, will change who they are. They will lose friends, family, loved ones and even their own soul. Their lives will be intertwined in a chaotic, uncontrollable world of greed. And when they are hurting, they too will inflict pain upon others.

Because of these fears and countless others, people have resigned themselves to the comfort of what they call, waiting on God. They decide to wait until they receive a clear sign from God or He delivers the package to their door. As a result, these people live and die in a hopeless state of passivity. All of their dreams, visions, and uniqueness go to the grave with them having served no purpose to mankind or God. The very purpose for which God created them goes undiscovered and unfulfilled.

Low Self-esteem

This may be one of the greatest areas that has an affect on the ability to achieve success for most people. Through years of oppression, many individuals have had their self-image desecrated so badly by people around them, they can't possibly believe anything great could ever ascend from their lives. They doubt that they are people of purpose who are created in the image of God. They doubt that God made all of us beautiful and unique to complete His will on earth. Because of past experiences and words that were spoken over their lives by people who were supposed to love and protect them, they have allowed fear, doubt and disbelief to enter and dominate their mindset.

Negativity is powerful. All it takes is a single word, malicious statement, or callous phrase from someone to eliminate dreams and destroy hope for many. Once doubt infiltrates your mind it will impede or stop your progress. You will ask who am I to even have such a dream? No one will want to hear what I have to say. People will consider my idea to be stupid. That's not my world. I won't even know what to do when I get there. I won't fit in. These are only some of the many excuses that people use as justification for not reaching beyond the boundaries. Through some form of covert oppressive operation, others created the boundaries. It's up to each of us to seek an answer to our dilemma and ask God for deliverance through His grace and mercy. For some of us, a psychologist cannot fix the emotional damage. It will take the power of the Holy Spirit and the word of God to set us free to enjoy the life God intends for us.

I am the youngest of five children. I was born out of wedlock when my mother was forty-years-old. I knew I had a father somewhere but I didn't know him. My first memory of my father was at the age of five when he promised me a bike. I never saw him again until I was sixteen-years-old.

Growing up with my mother wasn't easy. My siblings as well as other kids teased me because I looked different to them. I remember being told that my mother got me out of the garbage. My grandmother, grandaunts and uncles would call me the "bastard child." It wasn't easy for me to hear and it truly hurt me to some degree. Positive communication and the words "I love you," were never used around our house. Expressions of love, such as hugging remained nonexistent. My mother was abrasive in making it a point to remind me of her disdain. She'd say, "I didn't kill you," meaning, have an abortion, and that at least, "I'm feeding and clothing you." To her, that was enough. I was beaten almost daily and told that I looked like my "no good pa."

After a while, her words no longer pierced my heart as much as they did when my mother told me at the age of twelve that I would be "a nobody" and "nothing more than a prostitute." Her hate filled words cut through me like a razor sharp knife. In fact, I cried because of them for years. It destroyed my self-esteem, perception and what little hope I had for the future. My father issued a public disclaimer stating that I was not his child and my mother; well she had no faith in me. I didn't believe I had any reason to live. I contemplated and prepared to commit suicide at the age of twelve. I didn't want to live anymore because the one person I was living my whole life to please was incapable of loving me enough to protect me. Proverbs 18:4 says, "The human spirit can endure a sick body, but who can bare a crushed spirit?" My spirit was crushed. My escape came by delving into the silent world of books. I read anything I could get my hands on and copiously fed my mind with passion. Academically, I excelled and despite the state of affairs at home I completed high school at the age of fourteen. I was then forced to repeat another two years of high school because no one knew what to do with me since we were poor. I didn't know there was such a thing as college at the time or that it was a viable option. I wasn't privy to having knowledge about things that would help shape me into a stronger and wiser individual.

Through all of my trials, God had a plan. When I was fourteen an evangelist came to town. I went to listen because there was nothing else to do. He singled me out and told me that God had called me to ministry. He said that God's proof to me, of this calling, was that I'd be successful in school and in whatever career I selected. He looked into my eyes and said, "You will not die until you serve the Lord and you will be successful."

I allowed those powerful words of inspiration to infiltrate my soul and then fuel it. They helped me overcome the abuse I experienced in my past and those I'd surely encounter in the future. The battle was in my believing that God would keep His word versus the negative things people were speaking over my life daily. In the end I chose to believe God. Philippians 4:13 states, "For I can do everything through Christ, who gives me strength." This became my daily inspiration. I repeated it over and over again. I remained diligent in reading the word of God. I learned of His promises and hugged them so tightly that not even the pains from my past or internal wounds could pluck them from me. Ultimately God used me to lead my mother to the Lord before she passed away in 2004.

In an interestingly comical twist, I developed such a positive view of the world and myself that I became the opposite of what people thought about me. I evolved into an extremely self-confident and socially interactive individual. My nickname amongst friends was "Social Butterfly" and I wore the hat well. Amazingly, I was so sure of myself I never noticed I weighed over three hundred pounds. Every day when I got dressed to leave my house, I looked in the mirror and saw the person I called the "Sexy Beast." In my eyes, I saw myself as the most beautiful woman in the world and regarded men as fortunate if they got my attention because I was the best thing since raised bread. I had an active dating life with men of different races and professions. I was gorgeous and in charge of my world.

One day I decided to see my doctor because I was getting tired in the afternoons and my productivity had decreased. When the nurse weighed me, I immediately jumped off the scale and started ranting. I wanted to know how she could have me weighed on a malfunctioning scale. I demanded that she repair the scale, make sure it was calibrated and then have me weighed again. Despite my anger the nurse remained calm. She obliged me by touching the scale but really didn't do anything to it. Having calmed down, I got back on the scale and had to face the reality that I was nearly three hundred and fifty pounds. What a blow to my self-esteem. I was so self-absorbed; I didn't even notice I had gained all that weight. Being the positive and optimistic person I am, that lasted about two weeks and then I went to work to fix it. But, not before fussing at all of my friends for not telling me I needed to lose weight so I could correct the problem. I realized they loved me for whom I was. The problem was I wasn't as healthy as I needed to be. Facing reality helped me to make positive and necessary changes in my life. A friend gave me a hug and gently said, "I love you and it's all in the right places." The Sexy Beast was back!

When my environment and the people around me said I wouldn't amount to anything, God through His grace and mercy said "... I know the plans I have for you. They are plans for good and not for disaster, to give you a future and a hope" (Jeremiah 29:11).

Regardless of what you've done or are going through, God still has a plan for you. He wants to do something through your uniqueness that only you can do. Don't let anyone or anything steal that joy away from you.

Lack Of Understanding Of The Word Of God

To fully understand and embrace the benefits of the covenant of peace, one must also understand the desire of God to bless His people beginning back in the book of Genesis.

In the Garden of Eden, Adam and Eve were told they could eat of any fruit in the garden except one. As the story goes, the serpent deceived Eve into eating the fruit, which she eventually gave to Adam who ate from it. God then comes for His afternoon chat with the couple only to find they were afraid to come out of hiding because they were naked. The deception is revealed and God made harsh, life changing judgments on the serpent, Eve and then Adam.

To the serpent He says, "And I will cause hostility between you and the woman, and between your offspring and her offspring. He will strike your head and you will strike his heel" (Genesis 3:15). Hence the battle between the powers of darkness and the children of God began.

To Eve, God says, "I will sharpen the pain of your pregnancy, and in pain you will give birth. And you will desire to control your husband, but he will rule over you" (Genesis 3:16).

And then God speaks to Adam, "Since you listened to your wife and ate from the tree whose fruit I commanded you not to eat, the ground is cursed because of you. All of your life you will struggle to scratch a living from it. It will grow thorns and thistles for you, though you will eat of its grains. By the sweat of your brow will you have food to eat until you return to the ground from which you came. For you were made from dust, and to dust you will return" (Genesis 3:17-19).

This was the first time man was about to experience famine or poverty. In the Garden of Eden that afternoon, the stage was set for man to go through life experiencing deprivation. Deprivation manifested in the form of:

Spiritual separation from God: man had sinned and could no longer connect with the heart and mind of God. He no longer knew the hopes, dream, promises or intent of God.

Physical separation from God: God no longer returned to walk in the garden in the afternoon. So the comfort of God's presence and the calmness of His voice were gone.

Psychological turmoil: he now had to live with the guilt of choosing to disobey God rather than correct his wife. He had to deal with the shame of knowing that his own weakness had caused him to lose his dominion as ruler of God's creation. Without his leadership, the animals became wild and untamed. Hence, the prey and the predator.

Loss of bountiful provisions of food to eat: He now had to work the ground by tilling the soil, planting seeds and waiting for his crop to produce a harvest which he would then have to reap. Life went from easy to extremely hard instantly.

What's interesting is that God never cursed the man or the woman. He cursed the serpent and sent it to crawl on its belly for the rest of its life without any hope of redemption. But when it came to the man and woman, He did not curse them. He told the woman He would increase her sorrow but He never said she was cursed. When He spoke to the man, He never told the man he was cursed either. Instead, He said, "cursed is the **ground** for your sake ..." Why is this so important? If God had cursed the man or the woman, from that point on there would have been no hope of them ever being blessed. The work Adam would have put into planting crop would have been futile because he would not have been able to reap the blessing of a harvest. So it is important to note, that even though God placed a curse on the ground causing man to have to work to eat, He did not curse man himself. This makes it possible for blessings to be available in man's future.

Another important point to note in Genesis 3:18 is when God cursed the ground, He said "It will grow thorns and thistles for you..." Every time man went to work the fields, he was reminded of the curse by the evidence of the thorns and thistles. He was reminded daily that his life of labor was set by God and there was no way to change it.

Over the generations, man has used the phrase "By the sweat of your brow, you shall eat bread." This phrase serves as a constant reminder of an act of disobedience to God. We are still working hard to meet our needs in these modern times. Sadly many Christians use this along with other scriptures to ferment the concepts that God did not intend for us to be bountifully blessed.

When reading scriptures such as Ecclesiastes 5:19-20 "... it is a good thing to receive wealth from God and the good health to enjoy it. To enjoy your work and accept your lot in life – this is indeed a gift from God," it does little to motivate Christians into believing wealth and health comes from God.

Wealth was not possible unless it came from God. In Deuteronomy 8:18 God reminds the people to not only remember Him but also that "He is the one who gives you power to be successful, in order to fulfill the covenant he confirmed to your ancestors with an oath."

However, Luke 6:38 says, "Give, and you will receive. Your gift will return to you in full—pressed down, shaken together to make room for more, running over, and poured into your lap. The amount you give will determine the amount you get back."

How is this possible? God cursed the ground back in Genesis and told man that he would have to work the ground in order to be blessed. How can I expect to receive a harvest of something I did not work for?

First of all, in Genesis, God said you would eat from the ground but He did not say your labor would produce a blessing like it says in Luke 6:38. If God intended for us only to have the results of our labor, then this scripture need not be applicable to the laborer. The blessing of an open heaven would also not apply.

"Bring all the tithes into the storehouse so there will be enough food in my Temple. If you do, says the Lord of Heaven's Armies, "I will open the windows of heaven for you. I will pour out a blessing so great you won't have enough room to take it in! Try it! Put me to the test! Your crops will be abundant, for I will guard them from insects and disease. Your grapes will not fall from the vine before they are ripe," says the Lord of Heaven's Armies, Then all nations will call you blessed, for your land will be such a delight," says the Lord of Heaven's Armies" (Malachi 3:10-12).

So how did we receive the ability to enjoy bountiful increase in our lives? God promises the increase under the covenant of peace when He said He would produce bumper crops. You do the work and God produces the increase.

Lack Of Understanding To Prosper And Expand The Kingdom Of God

There is a story in the Bible of a man who knew how to save a city that had come under attack. He knew the way in which the city could escape harm but no one listened to him because he was poor. Often in today's society the wisdom of the poor is despised because of the lack of finances. Not because the person doesn't have knowledge or understanding but because of the lack of money. Society associates money with power and influence. You can be deemed a fool with nothing relevant to say but if you have financial success, the world will listen to you.

Generations of Christians have gone silently to their graves without the influence they could have achieved if they acquired the finances to establish the credibility of the words of God. They preached and spread the gospel of a loving God who owns cattle on a thousand hills, has all of the power in heaven and earth and wants to bless us and keep us safe from our enemies. A God who gives man the power to get wealth so His covenant can be established on this earth (Deuteronomy 8:18). Yet, in their personal lives, they were constantly defeated by poverty. They struggled to meet their basic needs, fell short on education and failed to influence the world about the greatness of God because their lives did not represent what they preached. Who wants to serve a God that seems comfortable to let you live impoverished and underprivileged? What would be the benefit of serving such a God? Hearing what God can do is different from seeing what God can do.

Over the years, legislature has been passed in America that goes against the very foundations upon which this country was built. Christians have watched in a state of seemingly hopelessness as the Bible was taken out of schools along with many other new laws. Each activist group pushed their agendas and gained the attention of the government through numbers and finances. Meanwhile, the body of Christ sat in meetings trying to figure out how to raise funds to send missionaries into the world and pay off their ever-looming debts. Additionally, they lacked finances to support agendas that brought God to the nations or ensured what this country was built on, remained intact. Hence, Christians have been forced into the sidelines of influence and power, silenced by their adversaries by nothing more than the lack of financial strength. Christians watch from the sidelines as the media preferentially chose Christian ministers to speak on certain topics because they won't be controversial on matters that are occurring in society. What was once a strength has now become an avenue in which Christians are mocked and pushed aside.

Some Christian leaders who have made it to a place of influence through finances and the vast expanse of their ministries have managed to reach the world with the gospel, won souls for Christ and have established that God definitely wants us to be blessed. It takes money to take this message to the world regardless of what stream you choose to use.

On the other hand, there are those who achieved immense success in their ministries, have great influence but have managed to turn so many people off from God through their personal focus on self. Their money, power and influence is more about them and promoting their personal agendas rather than it being about looking after the lost and helpless people of this world.

The point is that without some measure of success in your financial life, you will not have the power or influence to make changes in this world. As Christians, we are accountable to God to know His word, apply it to our lives and allow God to give the increase to what we have sown. We are responsible to know what is happening in society and be equipped to influence the changes that are necessary.

Without money, power and influence we are left to silently suffer through the decisions that are made for us by persons who may not know God or persons who despise the very mention of God or the Bible. This is evident today through the many laws that have been put in place to protect the rights of so many while Christians are now being victimized and stereotyped into people or group haters.

In the book of Ecclesiastes 10:19 it says, "... money gives everything." In other translations money is referred to as the answer to all things. I have a tendency to believe what the Bible says despite the fact that many will argue with this statement. Over the years, I've come to realize that while money cannot buy happiness, it provides opportunities to pursue the things or people that bring joy into our lives. Money allows you to pursue the best educational opportunities without having to wait for a favorable reply from a scholarship committee or another person to be merciful to you. Please note that I am not degrading these avenues but the freedom to choose where and how you want to be educated is primarily determined by the extent of your financial strength.

As a health care professional, I have seen numerous people being turned down for beneficial treatments because of lack of finances while others are able to indulge in selective health amenities due to the size of their wallets. To get to the bottom of the matter, most Christians can't afford quality food, prescription medications or even nutritional supplements because of lack of finances. As a result, their health gradually decline and most die of diseases that are preventable. Had the finances been available to them, they would have access to the best health care, quality food, prevention programs and would have been able to maintain a healthy long life.

I have no doubt that finances directly affect health. In addition to the inability to afford proper health care and food amongst other things, our emotional state is also directly affected. A man who cannot adequately provide for his family will experience emotional issues. Women who watch as their children suffer from starvation are also emotionally troubled by this experience. What we have seen happen in many societies is that some of these people have turned to illegal means to be able to provide food and clothing for their families. Sex, drugs and alcohol have dominated as top earning avenues for many people. It comes at the expense of lives being destroyed and a society that is thrown into chaos. Children are being left alone to raise themselves while parents are out struggling to keep food on the table. Hence, our ability to raise children to prepare them for a future filled with hope is severely impaired.

The church that is supposed to be a place to get people back on track cannot help because it too is struggling under the weight of heavy mortgages, operating expenses and inadequate resources to influence change. People have become discouraged and despondent in the midst of their hopelessness.

It is imperative that Christians understand and accept that we have a responsibility to prosper. God gave us a mandate to take care of the poor, widows and orphans. He also, commissioned us to make wise decisions with what He has given to us.

In the parable of the rich man who went away and gave three servants different amounts of money, there is a lesson to be learned. At the end of it all, the rich man was pleased with the two servants who multiplied what was given to them. However, the Bible does not say what each of them did to receive the increase. But the third servant who did nothing with what was given to him was called wicked. Here we are told what he did with his share. He hid it and waited for the rich man to return using the excuse that he was afraid of what the man would do if he lost the money. Excuses! Excuses! Excuses!

Many of us are like that wicked servant. God has already given us an opportunity to invest and grow but we have hidden our talents and resources under the seat of moral and spiritual passivity. "Well, I don't want to be like these rich, greedy people. Money changes people and I don't want to be anything God would not be pleased with." Some say, "If I give this away or even invest this, I won't have enough for myself or family and I will not be deprived." What we don't realize is that God will eventually take all that we have set aside if we fail to invest and make His blessing in our lives multiply.

Another interesting point to note is that God took what the wicked servant had and gave it to the servant who already had the most. He did not give it to the servant who multiplied his three talents into six. He gave it to the one that demonstrated he could handle a greater allocation because God realized that the servant had the right heart and the ability to increase no matter how much was given to him.

Without wealth and health, it is impossible to change the world for Christ. It is time for Christians to realize that the only way God's covenant of peace can be fulfilled on this earth is through our willingness to be the vessels through which He gives the increase.

By becoming vessels of integrity and honor, God can now use us to be game changers for His kingdom. "May your Kingdom come soon. May your will be done on earth, as it is in heaven" (Matthew 6:10). We can experience a piece of heaven while here on earth. We are responsible to make whatever God gives us to work with, increase in our lives so when the time of harvest comes, we reap a bumper crop of influence, honor and wealth.

Chapter Nine

Dare to Believe

Can you dare to believe that God loves us so much that He placed many checks and balances in His word to allow us to overcome every obstacle that would attempt to keep us from His blessings? God knew, even before we were created, that we would fall short in our human form. He created opportunities from Genesis to Revelation for many to overcome through perseverance, obedience, and faith in Him. The main requirement is that we believe God is able to do what He says He will do. Faith, having hope and trust in God, is the first and most important step to living under the covenant of peace.

The argument has been made that people who don't serve God have prospered tremendously and achieved great wealth and influence. Yes, this is so for the mere reason that if God gives an instruction with a promised outcome, whomever implements the principle will receive the reward as God says because His word does not change.

When Jesus spoke of the parable of the rich man and his three servants, there was no mention of whether or not these servants were believers in God or Jesus. The only thing mentioned is what they did with what was given to them. Under the covenant of peace, God is saying that He will increase you. Your harvest will be greater than any others. This should get you excited because if the greatest achiever in your area of expertise was a non-believer in the word of God, you should be expecting to make history. You should expect to break records, set a new trend for success. Your achievements would now become the blueprint for success. Through no human effort, your harvest is expected to be exceedingly larger than anyone else and infamous. I often wonder what the success level would be like if many of the world's most wealthy, powerful and influential people had a heart and passion for the things of God. What we see as the pinnacle of success would have been dwarfed by what God would have really done. It may have cost them less time, energy and sacrifice. Or it may have given them more joy and peace in life. I don't know but I think about it and wonder how much more God could have improved on human effort.

The Bible demonstrates that we must believe that when we plant a field, we will reap a harvest. It's imperative that we do our part. Yes, give tithes and offerings but also plant seeds into others and most importantly, into yourself. Invest in education of knowing God and advancing your knowledge in your area of specialty. If you're already in a profession, seek to excel in your specialty. Learn all you can and conduct yourself with integrity. Someone is watching you as you plant those seeds of trustworthiness, reliability, dependability and self-motivation. When the time of harvest comes, God will place it in the heart of your employer to reward your diligence with promotions and salary increase.

As an entrepreneur, take the time to learn all you can about the market you are targeting. Learn your business model, vision and mission. Sow daily into increasing your visibility in the market. Attend business seminars and events. Interact with others of similar interests. Seek healthy relationships and resources. At the right time, God will plant your name and product into the heart of someone through whom God will change your life forever.

To the homemaker, the stay at home mother or father. Invest daily into teaching your children the ways of God. Teach them good morals and values. Spend time with them and give them all the love God has generously placed inside of you. Take time to affirm your children so they already know who they are and why they are created before they enter the world. Instill strong principles of how to maintain healthy relationships with others of different cultures, race and belief systems. Teach them about money, its importance and how to manage their finances. Enlighten them about making healthy food choices that would allow them to maintain the vessel God has given them for this earthly journey. At just the right time, God will bring to remembrance what they have been taught and guide them through their lives based on your investment. You may be raising the next John the Baptist, Paul, or even the next most influential person in the world. Your harvest will be what you have invested.

The world has been changed through inventions. Inventors have the responsibility to develop the ideas that God has placed inside of them. Seek ways to get your product to market and begin by believing that you can. Seek audiences with persons who can assist you to do what needs to be done. God will give you favor with someone who will embrace your vision and take it to the world.

To the politician to whom God has given a platform to influence nations and even the world, know the agenda of God and stick to it. Don't compromise on your integrity and morals. Hold fast to what you know to be truth according to the word of God and make sure you push for what is right in the eyes of God. In time, each of you will have the ability to make changes that will be heard around the world. You will leave a legacy that affects the lives of many.

Ministers and leaders, God is prophetically promising that if you don't lead with diligence and integrity being mindful to carry out His mandate regarding people placed under your care, He will remove you from your position. He will take away your rights to leadership. King Saul, in his disobedience, died a disgrace on the battlefield. You have the power to turn your situation around. Follow the plans of God. Invest daily in studying the word of God. Be prepared to teach your followers as God opens and enlightens your mind and heart to His word. Be prepared to lead the sheep God places under your care with fervor, honesty and integrity. Take the time to invest in your members to ensure they are equipped to become what God has designed for them. Let failure be their choice rather than your neglect. Remember God gave you the ministry and He will also tell you who is to replace you. Be honest with yourself and examine whether the child you so desperately want to be your successor, has the heart and passion for it as you do. Don't force your children into the position of faking it until they hopefully make it. It will destroy your legacy. Be sensitive to the people God has placed in your environment and ask Him to guide you as to who should be your successor. Invest daily in your replacement so your legacy will continue as promised in Psalms 112:9. Be willing to recognize and accept that your replacement may not necessarily be your child but the individual who embraces your vision with passion and is willing to receive from you while obeying the voice of God. King Saul, chosen by the people, disobeyed God and died without leaving a legacy. King David, chosen by God, became the greatest king to rule over Israel. He died leaving a legacy of obedience and passionate love for God. Through his lineage, Christ entered the world. God will give you sustainable increase in your ministry, influence and power. Like Paul, you will be able to say, "I have fought the good fight, I have finished the race, and I have remained faithful" (II Timothy Chapter 4:7). You will finish strong and with integrity.

Chapter Ten

How We Know! How We Move!

We are destroyed by our lack of knowledge. Not the lack of health, relationships or finances. By reading this book, you have begun a journey of knowledge that will lead you to your desired outcome. It is my prayer that God will use this book to be the start of the next phase of your life. It will be a life that is filled with the presence and abundance of God. You will experience the covenant of peace in your daily life. And, when you come to the end of your time here on this earth, you will have completed all you were designed to do, trained your replacement and left a legacy for generations to come.

I encourage you to develop a lifestyle designed for success. Below are a number of recommendations to help you begin the incredible relationship with your heavenly father.

1) Daily enter into communication with God. Read the Bible and mediate on its words. Ask God to open your understanding and knowledge of Him so you can fully comprehend the extent of who He really is to you. Don't be afraid to ask for guidance on matters you may not understand. Our experiences with God are unique to each of us. What others experience may not necessarily be what God wants us to experience with Him.

2) Rather than look for words and actions that fit into the life you want to live, apply yourself to the truth of God's word. When you discover parts of your life and belief system that does not match the truth of God's word, don't try to change the word to suit you. Make changes in yourself to match the word. One thing I've learned during my time with God is that it's impossible to experience the presence of God and not change.

3) Verify and validate the opinions and philosophies of people you allow to influence your thought process. Become accountable to yourself for the information you allow to shape your thinking. It will eventually shape your behavior and the outcome of your life. Simply look to God for answers and not to man. We are all fallible and subject to error. Don't base your entire life on the opinions of other people.

4) Develop a passion for learning. Make it a point to learn something new every day. Learning

new things will be like a breath of fresh air. It will energize and transport you into a private world of peace. Find contentment in knowing that no one can remove your knowledge and power.

5) Validate friendships and strengthen the ones who qualify for access to your environment. Be open to the possibility that people who are around you today are not necessarily meant to remain for the long-term.

6) Keep family and relationships in its rightful position as the number one priority (under God) in your life. Actively take part in activities that creates beautiful memories and strengthen emotional bonds.

7) Continue Moving in 3-D® (Desire, Determination and Discipline) towards a lifestyle of truth, integrity, education and health. Prosperity will accompany you. You will be planting a field that will produce an undeniable harvest of gratifying rewards. It will cause you to live victoriously rather than as a victim.

So, begin today on this incredible journey knowing that your Heavenly Father loves you! He wants you to prosper! He wants you to be a success! He wants you to experience a piece of Heaven while here on earth!

Journal your experiences so you can always remind yourself of the goodness of God!

May the blessings and presence of God be with you now and always; may the grace and peace of God rest upon your life. In Jesus' name I pray it is so, Amen!

About the Author

Shawn Saunders is an obedient woman of God, loving mother, friend and successful businesswoman residing in Florida. Shawn shares her incredible triumph over pain through faith and passion for God. Shawn reveals what some may not want you to know about the Covenant of Peace.

For speaking engagements or more information visit: www.shawn-saunders.com.

www.ingramcontent.com/pod-product-compliance
Lightning Source LLC
Chambersburg PA
CBHW071519040426
42444CB00008B/1723